FOLKLORE OF WALES

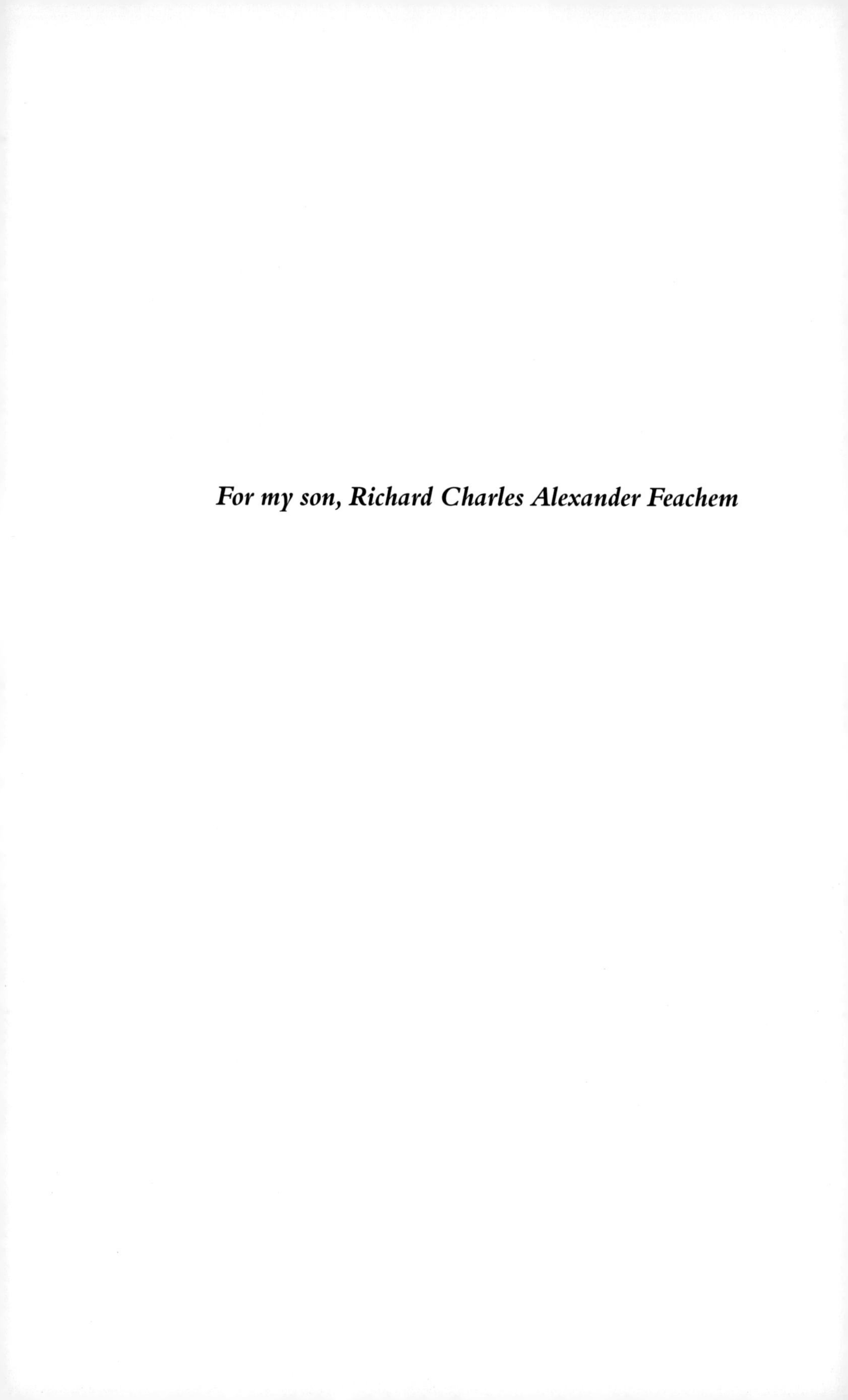

For my son, Richard Charles Alexander Feachem

FOLKLORE OF WALES

ANNE ROSS

TEMPUS

First published 2001

PUBLISHED IN THE UNITED KINGDOM BY:

Tempus Publishing Ltd
The Mill, Brimscombe Port
Stroud, Gloucestershire GL5 2QG
www.tempus-publishing.com

PUBLISHED IN THE UNITED STATES OF AMERICA BY:

Tempus Publishing Inc.
2 Cumberland Street
Charleston, SC 29401
1-888-313-2665
www.arcadiapublishing.com

Tempus books are available in France and Germany
from the following addresses:

Tempus Publishing Group
21 Avenue de la République
37300 Joué-lès-Tours
FRANCE

Tempus Publishing Group
Gustav-Adolf-Straße 3
99084 Erfurt
GERMANY

British Library Cataloguing in Publication Data.
A catalogue record for this book is available from the British Library.

ISBN 0 7524 1935 8

Typesetting and origination by Tempus Publishing.
PRINTED AND BOUND IN GREAT BRITAIN

Contents

List of illustrations

Acknowledgements

It is impossible to acknowledge all those who have encouraged me in one way or another in my research into the culture, past and present, of the lovely land of Wales. I must include the many Welsh people who have shared their own inherited folk traditions with me and especially the people of this region of mid-Wales where a great deal of folklore still survives and much of which still awaits collection. This I hope to do while memories of the past still remain amongst the older people and some of those of younger years. All my good neighbours must be thanked, and many Welsh friends from different areas of Wales. Perhaps the most generous of these is John E. Williams of Llanrug, himself a writer and a storehouse of old Welsh traditions, John P. Williams, Brother Gildas of Caldey Island, and countless others. My greatest inspiration comes from the wonderful works of my long-standing friend, Rachel Bromwich, whose magnificent study, *Trioedd Ynys Prydein* (The Triads of the Island of Britain) — a new edition of which is on the verge of publication — and whose generous sharing of her knowledge and loyal friendship to all has deeply enriched our understanding and enjoyment of some of the oldest literary traditions of Wales.

Each member of my family has contributed to the creation of this work. My husband Richard has added an extra dimension to the book with his fine maps and drawings, Berenice with her tireless expertise on the computer and in many other ways, and Charles by his own computer skill and ungrudging help in every aspect of our daily lives. To them all I extend my heartfelt gratitude.

Finally I would like to thank all the staff of Tempus, and Peter Kemmis Betty whose unfailing good humour and patience ease the inevitable stress of writing to a deadline and make the creation of books for Tempus a pleasure and an exciting venture.

1 Introduction

Wales is a Celtic country. Many of its people still speak, read and teach the language which has evolved from a branch of ancient Celtic known as Brythonic or P-Celtic, spoken widely on the continent of Europe long before Julius Caesar made his superbly-organised — and ruthlessly aggressive — conquest of the Gauls (*Galli*) in a series of hard-fought battles, terminating with the defeat in 52 BC of Gaul's greatest hero the Arvernian Vercingetorix ('Great King of Heroes'), who raised the revolt against Caesar. This famous Gaulish warrior was forced to surrender to the Romans and was subsequently executed in 46 BC.

It is instructive to cast one's mind back to this period of European history and the tribal organisation of the Celts in Europe because I believe that at this early period the seeds of the later post-Roman, Celtic world were sown; and many of its singular and unique characteristics originated even before the defeat of Celtic Europe. Much of what we learn of our continental forebears would seem to provide us with a plausible explanation of certain predilections which evolved into enduring motifs in the development of the rich oral literature of the British Isles. It is a strong possibility that Caesar's initial invasion of southern Britain in 55 and 54 BC — and the presence of a great number of soldiers recruited from the defeated Gaulish protagonists augmented by fighting men from various other outposts of the empire — began the process of moulding the indigenous Celtic traditions and reshaping them into new and perhaps more sophisticated forms.

By AD 70 Wales had become a vibrant part of the Roman Empire (**1**) and thus the rich early literary traditions of Britain contain many references to the new influences which inevitably appeared. As in all the Celtic countries, genealogy was of first importance and in Wales it was not unusual, as the people became habituated to the new order, to find Roman names being included in genealogical compilations as the initial hostility gave way to acceptance. The Celtic inhabitants of the Island of Britain might have been expected to feel continuing hostility and resentment towards their Roman conquerors whose basic attitudes and very thought processes were so alien to their own — and destructive of the native way of life. However, many benefits were to accrue. The Classical writers, while understandably proud of their military prowess, did make some important comments both in Gaul and Britain, on the nature,

1 *The Background to Wales. Central western Britannia before and after the arrival of the Roman armies. The pre-Roman names are those of the British tribes, with a selection of hill-forts [circle]. The names of the Roman period are those of the forts and fortlets established during the campaigns [square]. The principal roads are indicated*

appearance and customs of the insular Celts, and showed a considerable interest in Celtic beliefs and religious practices which deeply intrigued them. Indeed, some of these comments can actually help us — the present-day Celts — to understand who we are, from what we are sprung, and to provide us with fresh clues to some of the singular features of our native culture.

One of the most striking aspects of the insular Celtic world at all periods down the ages is the passion for learning, religious fervour — pagan, and then Christian — and a deep respect for the aristocratic and priestly leaders. Thinking about the singular survival of the oral traditions of all the Island Celts — and doubtless those in Europe also — it would seem that this distinctive and often quite remarkable facility for oral learning and recitation must stem directly from some archaic discipline imposed upon the then tribal structure of Celtic society at a very early period, perhaps even before the differentiation of the Welsh and Gaelic dialects (Brythonic and Goidelic). It is clear that the people responsible for this deep-rooted intellectual zeal must have been highly organised and educated themselves. Ultimately the chief of these, and the most influential, must have been the Druids, the Vates (prophets) and the Bards (poets). We would not know anything about these orders at such an early period had it not been for the invaluable records of the Classics: Greeks, with whom the Celts were originally at war, and later the Romans. Their accounts of these holy and learned orders and their enormous influence over the Celtic tribes are invaluable and vital for any understanding of both the religious attitudes in Gaul, and — after the Roman invasions of Britain — in this country also.

Of particular importance are the accounts of the Celtic passion for committing facts to the memory rather than relying upon the written word. The Romans moreover displayed a considerable admiration for the remarkable intellectual powers of the enemy. When Tacitus wrote his account of the invasion of Britain by Claudius, he commented upon the very important fact that while the young men of Gaul were extremely receptive of education, the young Britons were even more so (Tacitus, *On Britain and Germany*, p.72). The fact that these important comments were made by the Classics, combined with the information which is supported by all the insular sources — and the fact that Druids were common both to Gaul and Britain — perhaps provides the key to an understanding as to why oral traditions and oral recitation should be universally practised throughout the Celtic world.

Many oral traditions have been preserved by Celtic peoples who have settled as far afield as, for example, New Zealand, Patagonia, Nova Scotia and elsewhere, and frequently the preservation of oral fragments can help to fill lacunae in the older, indigenous, orally-transmitted literature. It is natural that the Celtic countries still speaking a Celtic language and possessing the most prolific material and the greatest range of subject matter should be given priority in our assessment of this unique heritage of oral material. Nevertheless we must not forget that important traces still remain in the tradition of other parts of the wider Celtic world in, for example, Cornwall, the Isle of Man, and even in parts of rural France and once-Celtic Europe. In this book we shall be concentrating upon the rich and varied folklore and storytelling repertoire of Wales.

2 Folk narrative

The Romano-British god Nodons, who appears in early inscriptions on stone, is reflected in the Welsh deity Nudd and must be cognate with the Irish god Nuadu. He is one of the many Irish deities who figure in and whose attributes occur in Welsh folklore. Many of the ancient gods of Britain and Ireland figure in Welsh mythology in the role of superhuman heroes. Fionn MacCumhail is another major Irish heroic figure of clearly divine origins whose popularity must have been almost as great as Arthur's over the whole European continent, and whose name appears in many Europaean place-names, as does that of Arthur the mythical king *par excellence* of Welsh tradition (**2**). The great question is: were such deities and heroic figures essentially an integral part of the Irish tradition and were they then borrowed, in some form, into the Welsh repertoire? Or, as I myself believe to be more likely, were they all gods and heroes at some early pre-textual stage of Irish and Welsh history thus common to both traditions?
(*vide* Rachel Bromwich, John Carey)

Belyn ap Madoc

Belyn was a prince of Merioneth — the name would seem to stem ultimately from the name of the ancient Celtic god Belinos who figures as Beli Mawr in the Mabinogion — and he had been perusing the Triads and pondered a long while upon one, namely:

> The three Blessed Astronomers of the Island of Britain — Idris, the Great; Gwydion, son of Dôn; and Gwyn, son of Nudd — they had a vast knowledge of the stars and of the ways in which they influenced affairs. They were able to foretell whatever anyone might wish to know till the day of judgment.
> (Trevelyan p.48ff)

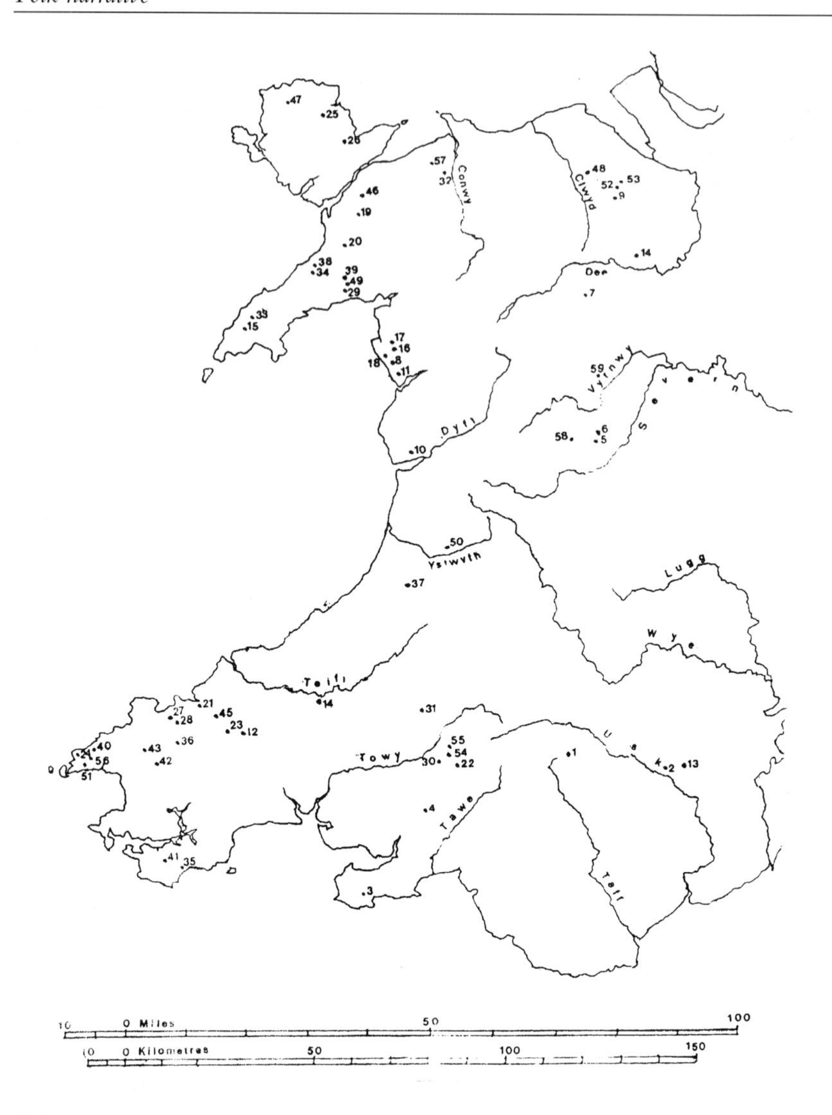

2 *Arthur in the names of natural features, ancient monuments and later buildings in Wales. For the most part after C. Grooms,* The Giants of Wales, *Lampeter, 1993*
1 and 2: Arthur's Chair; 3: Arthur's Stone; 4 to 8: Carreg Arthur; 9 and 10: Carreg Carn March Arthur; 11: Cerrig Arthur — *Arthur's Stones; 12:* Cerrig Meibion Arthur — *Stones of the Sons of Arthur; 13:* Cist Arthur — *Arthur's Chest; 14 to 43:* Coetan Arthur — *Arthur's Quoit; 44: Craig Arthur; 45:* Eisteddfa Arthur — *Arthur's Seat; 46:* Fynnon Cegin Arthur — *Well of Arthur's Kitchen; 47 to 51:* Maen Arthur — *Arthur's Stone; 52: Parcarthur Farm; 53: Parcarthur House; 54:* Pen Arthur — *Arthur's Hill; 55:* Pen Arthur Isaf — *Arthur's Small Hill; 56: Pen Arthur; 57:* Picel Arthur — *Arthur's Spear; 58: Arthur's* Wern — *Arthur's Alder Tree; 59:* Fynnon Arthur — *Arthur's Well*

He was particularly fascinated by the statement that this prophet could provide foreknowledge of anything until the day of judgement. Curious though he was, Belyn was not at all anxious to be able to foretell future events as far as the apocalypse. He seemed to be somewhat uneasy at this thought. What he really wanted to know was whether he would become famous and would be a great leader, as legendary as Owen Glendower. He sat and thought and then an old tale came to his mind: the tale of Cadair Idris, a long and impressive mountain round which the rivers Mawddach and Dysynni run, on the boundary between the old kingdoms of Gwynedd and Powys. The legend stated that whosoever should sleep for one night on Cadair Idris would either go mad or wake up having the gift of inspiration. It is not clear whether this was poetical inspiration or astrological inspiration but it is likely that it was both of these gifts, as, in Celtic tradition, prophets, poets and madmen, all of whom possess some degree of inspiration, are closely linked.

No matter which of these was imparted by the mountain, Belyn was eager to possess it and he immediately set out to find the right way of obtaining knowledge of the future. He had taken, as he thought, sufficient provisions to keep him going during his quest, and aimed to reach the summit of Cadair Idris soon after midday. It is a magnificent ascent — and is as beautiful and awe-inspiring today, being totally unspoilt. The road wends steeply upward from Dolgellau to become ever wilder and more dramatically hazardous. Below there were long tracts of rich pasture and the slopes were covered with the brilliant yellow of gorse flowers which make so striking an impact when seen against the bright green of the Welsh countryside.

At last Belyn reached the grand summit and was able to look over vast and dramatic tracts of countryside. He waited for some hours, contemplating various matters and gazing upon the dramatic beauty of the vista until the last rays of the sun blazed above the mountain tops and the day drew to a close. That was the time for Belyn to proceed towards Idris' Chair and there he sat himself down. Eagles flew above him and vultures gathered; kestrels and kites (*vide* **42**) circled in the air of the evening. Belyn began to feel that he was becoming quite isolated from the world about him. This is when he took his seat in Idris' Chair. It grew dark and there was a magnificent display of heavenly bodies which sparkled like jewels in the clear, darkening sky. He began to feel quite fevered and was filled with a terrible restlessness. When he felt himself becoming sleepy he tried to keep awake, fearing the magical sleep which he had come all this way to experience, and believing that he was going mad. A thick darkness fell and he felt a terrible sense of suffocation and terror come over him, and he also felt desperately ill, wishing that he had never set out on this foolish adventure. Then the darkness began to lessen and he saw a faint glimmering of light which grew pale enough to reveal the silhouettes of giants, and he began to think of all the legendary kings and heroes and especially the Grey King (*Brenhin Llwyd*) who was reputed to sit amongst the mountain tops to discover the secrets of the stars.

Next Belyn heard sounds like those of great flood waters being released; what with the noise of the waters and of several winds competing with each other, he remembered the legend of 'the fountain of the waters and the cradle of the winds'. He imagined that the lightening of the heavens indicated that dawn was not far away, when he heard a voice which said 'When you have secrets do you know where to hide them?', and another, hollow voice replied 'No.' The first voice replied: 'Trust them to the depths of the sea; trust them to the strongholds of the rocky mountains; trust them to the distant lone star, not to a mortal being.' To Belyn it was a relief if not a pleasure to hear these unearthly voices. 'Are you ambitious?' asked the louder voice. 'Yes, yes', replied the quieter voice. It gave a cryptic reply, the gist of which was that too much ambition would end 'in conflict, in death, in dust!'. Then another voice intoned, saying that few people win fame, the monarch may have his crown but it would cause him pain, the warrior his strength but that must leave him eventually, and will have been in vain. Belyn's heart sank. As we know, it was his ambition to be like Glendower (*c*.1354-*c*.1416) and to become a great leader, a renowned warrior and to be famed throughout the wide world. As he sat gloomily one of the strange people seemed to read his thoughts, because after a few moments the greater voice cried:

> Take care, hasty youth, keep clear of warfare, of fighting, of sorrow, while there is time. As yet there is no single thread of silver hair amongst your dark and curling locks. We know what you want. You want to go out into battle, to earn a great name, to return to your home full of victory and triumph. But do not be hasty. There are many who will go down that road but few will come back. I say to you, go home and do not try to learn the secrets of the stars. The greatest thing for you is to be caring to your neighbours, as good to them as to yourself; to be true to yourself and to all mankind; to help the helpless, to bring comfort to those who sorrow; to feed the hungry and to succeed in those aspects of life which you were born to.

Then the voice ceased.

The huge figures slowly vanished into the morning mists, and when Belyn roused himself the sun was high. He was cold and stiff and aching after the night he had passed in the Chair of Idris. He began to turn over the events of the night: what had happened during the unearthly happenings? had he dreamt the whole thing? He seemed not to have gone mad, but whatever had

3 *'A commission for holding an Eisteddfod at Caerwys, in 1568, is still in possession of Sir Roger Mostyn, together with the Silver Harp, which had from time immemorial been in the gift of his ancestors . . . This badge of honour is about five or six inches long, and furnished with strings equal to the number of Muses.' This commission is dated to 23 October in the ninth year of the reign of Queen Elizabeth (1558-1603). From T. Pennant,* Tours in Wales, *I, 1874, London, 463-7*

happened it had certainly taught him his lesson. He knew he would never again undertake such a dangerous and foolhardy exploit. Slowly but thankfully he descended the great hill and made for home. 'Where have you been?', asked some passers-by on the path down the mountain. 'I have been up to the highest point', he said. 'He's been praying' — some fellows taunted him but Belyn left them alone. A neighbour nearer home said: 'Have you been up amongst the eagles?'. Belyn did not answer.

Eventually he approached his home and now twilight was coming again, slowly from the west. He stopped to look back at Cadair Idris and his eyes sought the very upper-most peaks, and he had a vision of the grey giants once again standing there and looking with kindness down upon him. Their outlines were softer, and they were no longer objects of fear, but appeared to be holding out their arms as if in the act of blessing him. At length he reached the home of his father, the half-ruined strong-hold beyond Dolgellau. He once more became oppressed with his thoughts, for his home, which had been a noble fort during the reign of Edward I, displayed the traces of desperate resistance and inglorious defeat. Belyn then wondered if it were not preferable to live in peace and leave the vagaries of war to the brave, wild warriors of Wales.

Turning all this over in his mind, he suddenly heard sounds of revelry coming from the banqueting hall and the voice of Owain Cyfeiliog, the poet prince of Powys, reached his ears. It was a long speech in praise of battle which ended with: 'Fill the Hirlais drinking horn . . . and bring it to Tudwr, the Eagle of Battles . . .' Belyn was puzzled by all the noise and revelry, the sound of the harp (**3**), the voice of Gruffydd their harpist; and there were wild bursts of applause. (The Welsh, almost always famous for their love of music, customarily played three instruments, namely the harp, the pipe and the crwth — a lyre-like instrument played with a bow.) There was a pause as he went on and because he did not wish to be seen he kept to the shadows and sought the shelter of the garden entrance to the great hall. Gruffydd began to play the harp again and to sing further. Then, to calm down the warlike spirits he had stirred up by his first song, he started to play the harp again. Belyn heard his father's voice bewailing his absence and, overcome with emotion, he rushed into his father's arms. When all the greetings were over, Madoc whispered a word to the warrior beside him and placed his son's hand in the warrior's. Belyn was taken aback. 'My son, my only son,' said Madoc, 'I proudly give your hand and if necessary your life into the keeping of Owen Glendower.' Belyn was stunned — where now his dreams of peace? He had been, without any reference to himself, placed in the hands of Owen Glendower, who until recently had been his great hero. After various formalities he discovered that he was pledged to go wherever Owen went and to defend the leader of the great uprising against the English King Henry IV. When he sat down beside his father, the words of the grey giant on the hill rang in his ears. 'Many will go forward, but few will come back.'

Belyn was no coward, but here were his new dreams of a peaceful world shattered. Not because he wanted this to happen, but because his great father had an iron will. Then he thought of the grim giant who said: 'Do well in the walk of life to which you were born.' So Belyn, seeing that his hopes were dashed, then and there made a resolution to try to do his best in whatever situation he might find himself.

Time passed, and eventually the battle started. Terrible screams and desperate cries of the living, and the heart-rending groaning of those who were wounded and dying, combining with the clash of arms, destroyed the peace of the day, and as evening drew near the frenzy only increased. The sea alone was tranquil. Hardly a ripple disturbed the quiet surface of Cardigan Bay. Monks and friars went onto the battlefield as evening fell, to administer such aid and healing as could be given to those who were wounded, and comfort to the dying. Voracious eagles and starving vultures hovered near the site, ready to take whatever carrion was available, and ravens and hooded crows croaked and barked on the lonely seashore while waiting for flesh. In the front of the battle, Owen Glendower urged his men on, while the opposing hosts fought, fell, rallied and wavered as the overwhelming force of the enemy oppressed them. The scene was ghastly, as the evening sunlight fell across the field of battle. Harlech Castle was taken by Glendower; Belyn son of Madoc lay wounded among his comrades.

It was now two years since his father had given him over to Glendower and a life of warfare, and there was not a braver soldier in the field. Now he was wounded and thought he was dying. He found himself, with others, close under the castle where the grass was thick and the shadows were dark. He thought he had been there for nights instead of two hours, when a voice roused him from his semi-conscious state. It said: 'If you wish for shelter and comfort, follow me.' 'I cannot', replied Belyn, 'I cannot move; my wounds are too severe.' So the stranger said 'I will carry you', and Belyn found himself in the great arms of someone who had superhuman strength. It was a short way to carry him, and the stranger soon placed him in the warm, comfortable kitchen of an old farmhouse. Belyn was amazed at his good fortune but too badly wounded and weakened to ask any questions. In a few days the enemy had gone, and Glendower's men held the castle. When peace reigned again, and the wounded recovered or died on the field, Belyn was able to sit up and found he was in the house of a friend he had not seen since childhood. Gwilym ap Hywel had been his father's closest friend, who had left Dolgellau to inherit estates on Anglesey. However he had fallen upon ill times and had been driven to live in this farmhouse, peacefully, with his good wife and children.

A girl came into the room and asked her father when the stranger would be able to sit with them at mealtimes. Her father told Belyn that this was his small daughter Eluned, and promised that as soon as Belyn could get up Eluned would nurse him, like her mother who nursed the wounded and the sick. When Belyn was able to walk, Eluned helped him and the two became inseparable friends. Belyn was with the family for several weeks. After he left, Eluned pined for him and her parents knew she had fallen in love with Belyn, son of Madoc. In Madoc's stronghold there was great rejoicing at his only son's return, and when all the feasting was over his father told him: 'You shall no longer follow the great Glendower in war, but take a wife and remain here in peace.' Then he told his father about his love for Eluned and his father was in full agreement with his choice of bride. So Belyn, accompanied by a full retinue, went back to Harlech and asked Gwylim ap Hywel for his daughter's hand in marriage. When he took his bride home to his father, all were amazed and delighted at her charm and beauty. Belyn now was deeply grateful to his father, who had 'given him to Glendower', for otherwise he would never have met his beautiful Eluned.

Never again did Belyn allow himself to be concerned about the Triad which had set him on his journey to Cadair Idris, but he never forgot his experience on the mountain, nor the advice that the Great Shadowy Ones had given to him, 'Go home and try not to learn the secrets of the stars. The greatest inspiration is to . . . do well in the sphere of life in which thou wast born.' And so it transpired as we have seen.

In this story there are several elements or motifs which are common to all Celtic storytelling both early and late, and customarily based upon an oral original. There were many reasons for this. The Welsh, like all the Celts, were quick to learn and voracious for knowledge. As we saw in the introduction, this characteristic certainly goes back as far as the time of Julius Caesar, and earlier archaeological monuments testify to *them* at a period before written documents in the vernacular had become widespread. The Druids passed on their learning by word of mouth, as did the early bards, and this tradition was also current amongst those who tilled the land and did not have the benefit of a fundamental education. The storyteller would hold his audience enthralled as he recounted tales not dissimilar to the one above, lightening the load of heavy physical labour and bringing relaxation, humour and a great deal of knowledge to those who would otherwise be denied it. Perhaps the complexity of the oral tradition is more highly developed in the Gaelic countries but that is not to say that Wales did not at one time have its full share of this tradition, although it would seem that for many obvious reasons it suffered more from political upheavals, invasions and the development, for example, of extensive coal mining in the north and steel-working, as well as coal, in the south. There were many set motifs, as we have seen in the tales, and any deviation from the accepted pattern of storytelling would be immediately checked by the quick minds of the engrossed audience.

In *The Lady of the Fountain*, a tale about Arthur and many adventures, we learn that the king was at Caerlion in Usk. Arthur said that if the others did not object, he would like to sleep while he waited for his dinner, 'And for your part, you can tell tales, and get a stoup of mead and chops from Cei' (*Mabinogion*, Jones and Jones, p.155-6). And so they sat and ate their meat and drank their mead, and then one of them, Owein, said to Cynon, one of Arthur's men: 'Start thou with the most wonderful thing thou knowest.' 'I will' said Cynon, who then embarked on the telling of a long and complex tale. This was a somewhat more sophisticated milieu than that of the small farmer or cotter or crofter, but hardly less enjoyable, and the audience was clearly just as avid for tales as were the humbler elements of society.

In our story we have seen the emphasis laid on Triads and triadic utterances and this is reflected in every aspect of Celtic folklore and tradition. The number three from earliest times was sacred throughout the Celtic world and superstition and belief in the existence and powerful influence of supernatural beings and forces was again a commonplace. This Merioneth tale, the central figure of which is Belyn ap Madoc, shows how the hero's life is deeply affected and influenced by his reading of an enigmatic Triad which led to a somewhat unnerving adventure on the mountain, Cadair Idris. Here he encounters one after the other, three gigantic beings, grey and sombre. The gods are invariably portrayed as being of great size and they often counsel and advise mortals. Here, although the eager young man is given advice by each of these great men in turn, he is not destined to follow the advice of the last speaker — which is somewhat overlaid with Christian morality. He goes home determined to follow this advice, but fate has a different future in store for him, as we have seen.

Place-names

Archaeology is more and more relevant to our studies of past history and hypotheses about previous religions and cult practices. Almost every week some new object, group of objects or significant site is brought to light by one or other of the current archaeological techniques. It is not perhaps irrelevant then to consider one recent site discovered in an aqueous context on the marshy wilds of Holme Beach, Norfolk, where a circle of oak trees currently dated to the Bronze Age has as its central point a vast oak tree, the whole imbuing this watery wilderness with an eerie atmosphere. Because this enigmatic circle resembles the great stone circles — the most famous of which is, of course, Stonehenge on Salisbury Plain — it has become known as Seahenge.

One antiquarian, namely the renowned Thomas Pennant, travelled widely in Wales in the eighteenth century, recording his many and astute observations on the history, antiquities and folk customs of various periods. In the opinion of the 'celebrated and learned Mr Henry Rowlands', former vicar of Llanidan (**4**), many of the great standing stones and remains of stone circles — often in a poor state of preservation — were of druidic origin. Be that as it may, there is one circle which is perhaps of singular interest: the stones having a *cromlech* in the centre. Mr Rowlands believed that this was a great temple of the Druids, and that the whole was originally surrounded with a circle of oak trees which formed 'a deep and sacred grove'. Romantic though this may seem, the Seahenge arboreal circle with a central feature consisting of a vast oak tree may indicate that Rowlands was not in fact far from the truth. Some ancient holy places may indeed have consisted of circles of oaks as the Classics record (*vide* Ross, *Druids*). We might also bear in mind the great circle of oaks centred by a complete giant tree of the same species dated by dendrochronology to the first century BC. This remarkable structure, which seems incontrovertibly to have been a great temple or sanctuary, is situated on the summit of the low eminence in County Armagh known as Emain Macha, 'Macha's Twins'. The name refers to the cult legend of the goddess Macha who was associated with horses and horse-racing and

4 Llanidan old church, Môn. (top) Head on right of south door (bottom) Head on left of south door

is a focal point for superstition and legend of every kind down the ages (*vide* Ross, *Druids*). There were doubtless many other temples constructed of oak, traces of which have usually gone unrecognised until recent years.

One of the most pathetic and tragic medieval Welsh stories is that entitled *Branwen Daughter of Llyr*. Although the story is full of fascinating motifs, in the main it lies outside the scope of this book, but there is one episode which has, I feel, an important place here, and that is the tragic death of Bran the Blessed's sister Branwen. Branwen and the seven men who alone had survived the terrible battle between the Irish and the Welsh — in this tale which constitutes of one the Four Branches of the Mabinogion (*Pedeir Ceinc y Mabinogi*) — made for Anglesey (*Ynys Môn*) carrying Bran's severed head with them. They came ashore at Aberalaw and sat down to rest. Branwen looked over the sea towards Ireland where her only child had been murdered by the Irish and gave a great sigh and her heart literally broke in her breast. Her companions constructed a four-sided grave for her on the bank of the River Alaw and here they buried her, and it has been known thereafter as *Bedd Branwen*. A few years ago, some excavation was done in what was believed to be the site of the grave but the only tomb that was discovered dated to the Bronze Age and so was discounted. However, I think this was not necessarily a piece of negative evidence. Tales about places linger long in remote rural areas and the storyteller of the Branwen legend may well have known that an important burial had taken place but at a period earlier than the story suggests.

3 Calendar customs

As we shall see throughout this book, the influence of nature and its vagaries have been, from earliest times down to the present day, prime factors requiring propitiation and offerings. The early Celtic year was — as it has remained, down to the present time — divided into four quarters, 1 November, 1 February, 1 May and 1 August, and each quarter was marked by a different celebration (*Calan Gaeaf*, *Gwyl Fair*, *Calan Mai* and *Gwyl Awst*) in keeping with the nature of the work. For example, casting lots for the fishing banks in regions where fish was a staple of the chancy diet. The period of sowing the crops in spring was likewise a time of hazard and anxiety, the success of the harvest being dictated right up to the last moment by not only the elements — and the good or ill will of the gods and malign forces of various kinds — but by the destruction of a splendid and seemingly safe grain crop, even on the eve before harvesting was due to begin, by sudden, violent storms and floods of rain causing the crop to be lost virtually overnight. This of course could and did lead to lack of food supplies for both man and the animals, resulting in sickness and disease and a high mortality rate. No wonder then that it was considered vital to propitiate the gods with sacrifice and offering and to enact the battle between the treacherous deity and the powerless farmers.

Thus in the Celtic countries, as widely elsewhere, plays representing this annual battle, literally between good and evil, were enacted by members of the communities concerned. Furthermore, by enacting the battle between good and evil, failure or success, it was believed possible to influence the actual outcome. The gods — and later God — must be offered their share of a successful season of whatever was taken or caught according to the nature of the harvest. From these simple rites of propitiation and fulsome acts of thanksgiving when all was safely gathered in, much of our surviving folk tradition is derived.

All the above comments are equally relevant to the traditions of Wales. As is the case throughout the British Isles, it was vital not only to keep a careful watch over crops and stock, but to play a full part in the thanksgiving which in post-Christian times took place within the hallowed precincts of the many ancient churches and in those built at a more recent date.

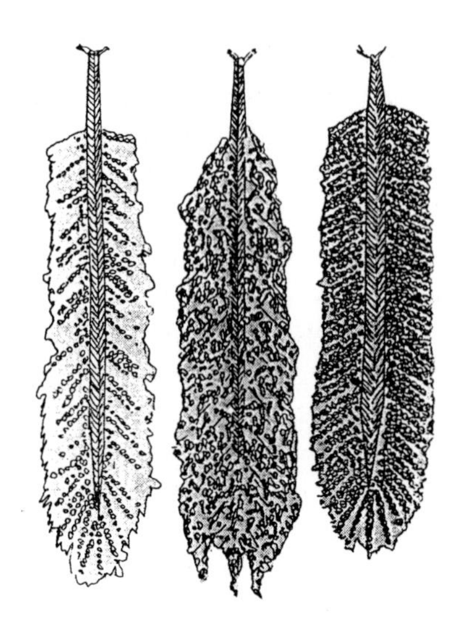

5a Caseg Fedi, *Barley, oats, wheat. From Llangynllo, Radnorshire. After I.C. Peate, 'Corn Ornaments', in* Folklore, *vol.82, 1971, pl.II*

5b Corn dollies, made from the last sheaf at harvest time. On the left, the caseg fedi, *after T.M. Owen* The Customs and Tradions of Wales, *1991, 13. On the right, a comparable Barley Maiden from Scotland*

The custom of the Last Sheaf was widespread in the scattered arable regions of Wales, many of which were extremely fertile. The Last Sheaf to be cut was treated with special honour, often being decorated in various ways, sometimes taking the form of an anthropomorphic figure, known in the Scottish Highlands as *a' Mhaighdean* if the harvest had been a good one and *a' Chailleach* should the harvest be poor or disastrous. A widespread tradition was to decorate it or tie it with coloured ribbons and hang it up in the kitchen of the farmer whose land had been harvested. There it held pride of place until the following spring sowing round about February when it was taken down and given to the horses to eat. The following year the same thing would happen. It was widely known as a corn dolly or a corn maiden but in Wales it was known as the *caseg fedi* 'harvest mare' (**5**) or *caseg hen fedi*, meaning 'end of the harvest mare'. In Welsh-speaking Pembrokeshire and the adjoining districts of south Cardiganshire and west Carmarthenshire, also in parts of Caernarfonshire, it was known as *y wrach*, 'the hag'.

The custom of the last sheaf is of great interest. Iorwerth Peate describes it from the information he obtained orally in different regions of Wales. Seemingly when the corn was being reaped, one patch was left in the centre of the field, uncut. Then the reapers came together with their sickles and the man in charge would go on his knees in front of the tuft of corn and divide it into three parts, plaiting these together as he would plait the tail of a mare. He would then secure the plaited clump a few inches above ground level. The eight or so reapers would stand some ten yards away from it, and each in turn would hurl his sickle at it so that it travelled just above ground level. The idea was to shear off the plaited tuft. If this was not achieved the chief reaper would then cut the tuft himself. As in Scotland, the harvest mare was taken to the farmhouse by the person who cut it, and there it would hang in the living room, to indicate that all the harvest had been reaped.

One informant told Dr Peate that, at a farm near Begeli in Pembrokeshire, he had seen 25 plaited sheaves in a single farmhouse, representing 25 years of harvest. The carrying of the plaited mare from the field into the farmhouse was not an easy matter. The household was warned that the last tuft had been cut, and planned to oppose it being brought into the house. If the bearer was anticipated as he was trying to enter the house he was 'rough handled' by the women and he had to place the plaited mare in a dry condition on the living room table. To prevent him succeeding he was often soaked with water or other available liquid. He usually succeeded by some clever trick. His companions, too, would help to foil the womenfolk in order to get the *caseg fedi* into the house, dry. If the reaper succeeded in this he had the place of honour at the harvest feast which followed. If he failed and the mare got wet it was not taken into the house. A mare that had not been soaked with water was an omen of good luck for a prosperous harvest in the coming year. In the same area, the successful reaper would shout out: 'In the morning, I got on her track, late in the evening I followed her; I've got her, I've got her.' He was then asked 'What have you got?', and he would reply, together with the others, '*Gwrach! Gwrach! Gwrach!*' (Hag! Hag! Hag!).

There were, of course, many variations on the details of this custom of 'taking in the mare'. In certain areas, for example in parts of Shropshire and Montgomeryshire, it was considered unlucky to celebrate the harvest home before all the harvest had been gathered in. I have certainly never heard of this happening in any of the Celtic countries in which I have collected harvest traditions. The bringing in of the last sheaf invariably symbolised the completion of the harvest. In parts of Denbighshire and Montgomeryshire, a miniature sheaf made of the ears and stalks was kept on the mantel-shelf until the following harvest. This may be compared with an east Pembrokeshire custom recorded in the 1870s of placing a small, poorly-executed specimen of the last sheaf in a small parcel and taking it at midnight to the neighbouring farmhouse.

There was, however, another custom associated with the reaping of the first sheaf. This was threshed with flails on the first day of cutting and the corn cooked to make a dumpling which was eaten at midday.

In parts of Cardigan the harvest pie (*poten pen fedi*) consisted of boiled potatoes and salt beef or bacon chopped together. These were put in a pot and cooked on a peat fire, peats also being put on the lid of the pot. For those further interested in these archaic and rather charming customs, they may like to know that the Welsh Folk Museum, which is at St Fagan's, not far from Cardiff, has several examples of corn 'dollies' from Wales, and is a treasure-house of other memorabilia.

When all had gone well and there was real cause for joyous celebration, special suppers were prepared for the workers, extra fodder and corn was given to the horses, and the stock and the *cwrw da* (good ale), for which Wales is famous, was imbibed while the local storyteller would be holding the close attention of those gathered together; songs of joy would be sung in the subtle style of old Welsh singing and the sweet music of the harp would further enhance the happy occasions. The brilliant Irish folklore scholar, the late Maire MacNeill, in her splendid study of *The Festival of Lughnasa* (1 August) has one or two comments to make about the *Lughnasa* gatherings in Wales which, as elsewhere, often took place on hilltops. *Lughnasa*, meaning the birth celebrations of the pan-Celtic god, Lugus, later Lugh, is an example of one of the many names of pagan Celtic divinities which in spite of Christian opposition, did survive in this country as elsewhere. The name given to this ceremony was often simply *Gwyl Awst* ('the August festival') and it became a regular Fair Day in some regions of North Wales. It is seemingly remembered likewise in central and southern Ceredigion, as a shepherd's Feast Day. This would seem to have become more or less redundant now, in so far as one can gather. To go back to *Gwyl Awst* in Ceredigion and North Wales, everybody would contribute some item of cooking or food, for example, a farmer's wife might lend a big kettle, and others would provide soup and sometimes everyone had to put a portion of the fuel necessary for the bonfire into the conflagration.

Little Van Lake

A mountain version of this 1 August celebration used to take place annually here. Great crowds of people, on the first Sunday in the month, went up the Brecon Beacons to approach Little Van Lake and watch for the appearance of the Lady of the lake at some time during the day. There was an interesting legend, which is related in full in chapter 9 *infra*, about this supernatural woman who used to appear briefly on this festive day.

The 1 August Mountain Assembly (*Lughnasa* in Ireland) *Gwyl Awst* in Wales was held widely in the British Isles in ever-increasingly vestigial form. Records of the Cornish traditions are extremely detailed as are those that remain in Brittany and in France. Maire MacNeill studied the Irish custom in her magnificent work and gives us tempting glimpses into the practices at this vital first fruit festival in other parts of Europe. One may infer that this ancient festival has, or certainly had, a very wide distribution throughout the whole of Europe, no matter what name was applied to it. To return to Wales, MacNeill, writing in 1962, makes the following comment:

> *Gwyl Awst* is now a day for fairs in certain parts of North Wales, and it is remembered in Central and Southern Cardiganshire as one on which the shepherds used commonly till comparatively lately, to have a picnic on the hills. One farmer's wife would lend a big kettle, and others would contribute, while according to another account, everybody present had to put his share of fuel on the fire with his own hands.
>
> But in Brecknockshire the 1st of August seems to have given way, some time before Catholicism had lost its sway in Wales, to the first holiday or feast in August, that is to say, the first Sunday in that month. For then crowds of people early in the morning, made their way up the mountains called the Beacons, both from the side of Carmarthenshire and Glamorgan: their destination used to be the neighbourhood of the Little Van Lake, out of whose waters they expected in the course of the day to see the Lady of the Lake make her momentary appearance . . . The story of the Lady of Little Van Lake, whom the Welsh pilgrims used till recently to go forth to see, is too long to be given here, and also too modern, in the form we have it, to clear up the details of the myth of which it forms a part.

(But see the Myddfai legend, chapter 9.)

Nos Calan Gaeaf (Hallowe'en)

Some customs seem to be based on working practices, others such as *Nos Calan Gaeaf*, or Hallowe'en are concerned with the home and the hearth which was an important focal point of all domestic life. This festival, which celebrates the approach of winter, the dark period of the Celtic year, took place on 31 October. It was held in all the Celtic countries, and is still remembered throughout the British Isles, and as far afield as America, Australia and New Zealand, where many Britons and other Celts have settled. It was believed that supernatural beings and powers became visible to mankind, that the graves opened and the dead walked again. Supernatural, hostile creatures also manifested themselves, such as the *Hwch Ddu Gwta* (the black, short-tailed sow). The *Hwch Ddu Gwta* frightened even the strongest of men. Pig-lore is very widespread in the Celtic countries and is particularly strong in Ireland and Wales. There is an enormous corpus of lore about pigs, pig transformation and great royal feasts at which the flesh of the pig was voraciously devoured. It was believed in the more northern parts of Wales that after the bonfire is turned into a smouldering mass, that the Black Sow made its appearance and would chase terrified young people, sometimes as far as their homes. I have heard that the Black Pig was particularly dangerous in the vicinity of the uneasy graveyard and the road led directly past this. The young people, and possibly some of older years, made a run for it in order to put behind them all the darkness and spectres as well as the Black Sow as soon as was humanly possible. My neighbour used to live in Bala and was very familiar with this tradition and the terrifying nature of the otherworld monster-pig.

The four calendar festivals in the Celtic world were basically fire-festivals. As the bonfire was sinking and turning into a heap of glowing ashes, it was a time when divination became clearer and the terrors of the night ahead drew near. I have a friend who lives locally who is a native of the country near the Lleyn Peninsula. He remembers how, as a boy, when the festivities were over and the fire was low and the young went on their way home in groups they really believed that the black sow was coning after them, and the greatest terror was to get safely past the churchyard with its own quota of horrors and reach home, running as fast as their legs could carry them.

The Welsh bonfires were taken very seriously, and the preparations for them were quite elaborate. Two or three would always be within sight of each other, and this brings to mind the hill-forts in the period of Roman occupation in Wales, when a beacon was lit on a prominent hill, for example Pen Dinas, Aberystwyth, and Pen Dinas, Elerch, some six miles apart, each one informing the other that danger was near. Everything combustible would be collected, for example huge quantities of straw, ferns, gorse and hawthorn bushes would be carted to the site; and as the fire was 'taking' there would be great noise from the blowing of horns and other instruments. People would dance and leap as the fire burned brightly, and roasted apples and potatoes would be eaten when cooked. My own memories of childhood Hallowe'en focus particularly on the delicious flavour of the potatoes when cooked in the bonfire, and taken out by the gardener to be split and filled with fresh farm butter as the fire began to sink. I think I have never tasted potatoes that were so fluffy and white and deliciously flavoured. We had the ghosts of the departed, but nothing so terrifying as the black short-tailed sow. There was usually some kind of celebration after the bonfires, held in one of the farmhouses. The traditional supper always included a mash-up of nine different vegetables which had salt and fresh milk added to make it nice and smooth. A wedding-ring was often hidden in the mash. The person who found the ring (hopefully not breaking a tooth on it first of all) was destined to be the first to marry, according to tradition.

A great vessel was filled with cold water and apples were floated in it and those present, who were able, got on their knees down on the floor and tried to bite one of the apples. Silver coins could also be used in this game and apples were hung by cord or string from the ceiling for a similar competition. We used to do virtually the same things when I was a child, but the apples were hung by a string from the pulley in the kitchen. Nuts also played a major role in the Hallowe'en festivities, and were roasted in the fire until they cracked and jumped out. Omens were read from where and how they landed. In the Welsh tradition, nuts and grains of wheat were placed in the fire and future events were read accordingly. Trefor Owen notes that in the Vale of Tywi, Carmarthenshire, young men used to bring pockets full of nuts to Hallowe'en parties and it was the custom to hand these round to the girls, old and young. Everyone took a turn at throwing a nut into the fire and watched closely while it burned; it was a matter of life and death — literally! If the nut burned brightly it indicated that the one who had cast it in would still be alive in 12 months' time. If a bright blaze did not occur then certain death awaited the one who had thrown it in. I think this game would probably best be avoided! Nuts were also thrown into the fire to see if the thing desired would in fact materialise, for example whether the girl or boy that the thrower loved would agree to marry the other.

A very important point on Hallowe'en was where two roads cross. This is always open to superstitious feelings and it was a place where spirits of various kinds were supposed to lurk. One of the more interesting customs noted by Owen was that at Tenby, Pembrokeshire, where it was a custom to sow hemp at a crossroads. The women performed this rite at midnight, having dug a small patch of ground. They would then chant, asking for the shape of their true love to appear, and rake the hemp seed after them. This is only one example of a widespread custom. Frequently it was carried out in a churchyard!

As in the Scottish Highlands, looking through the hole in a blade-bone of mutton was a way to prognosticate the future husband or wife, but unlike the Highland rite, nine additional holes were bored in it beforehand. Things could get somewhat out of control when men or young people went about demanding gifts from poor, frightened people. They would knock on every door, chanting strange rhymes and demanding gifts with a set rhyme. The youths, eager for treats, would go from door to door shouting '*Cnau ac afalau*' (nuts and apples). These were obtained especially for Hallowe'en ploys, and everyone received a generous portion. Sometimes rounds of the church were made and at one stage old rhymes were chanted but by the time leading up to the early twentieth century the ditties could be more or less meaningless.

The custom of 'souling' is a strange one correctly carried out on All Souls' Eve, 1 November, but there was confusion between All Hallows' Eve and All Souls' Eve, both of which were concerned with death and with the souls of

6 *The Antrobus Soulers, Cheshire, in 1972. After B. Shuel,* The National Trust Guide to Traditional Customs In Britain, *1985, p.179*

the departed. Part of the souling ritual took place in the parish church, that is, up to the eighteenth century, where in many areas candles were lit. These candles were donated by the parishioners. When they were lit, the way in which the flame burned, faintly or brightly, would serve as a prognosis of the future. This was not a very subtle procedure as, naturally enough, a brightly burning flame would indicate prosperity and presumably the wellbeing of the souls; a poor flame would suggest the reverse. If the candle were, however, to cease to burn before it had reached the candle holder, death within the year would certainly be the fate of the one who owned it. Once the last candle had been extinguished, everyone in the church walked three times round the building and then made for their homes, keeping total silence. In some ways, apart from the church ceremony, this would seem to differ little from the *Nos Calan Gaeaf* customs. The custom of souling was widespread in Wales and was extremely popular in the border counties of Cheshire and Shropshire. The cakes, which were specially made for the souling ceremony, were known as soul-cakes or dole-cakes (*pice rhanna* and *bara rhan*). Soul-cakes were regarded as being acceptable to the dead.

The height of the popularity of the festival was in the medieval period and prayers were offered up for the souls of relatives to be released from purgatory, should they have the misfortune to be in that gloomy place. Souling plays were very popular in Cheshire, but only three survived the Second World War, which did much to terminate many such traditions throughout the British Isles. The most famous of the Cheshire celebrations is the Antrobus Souling Play, which is still celebrated on All Souls' day or Hallowe'en. This is very popular and people come from a wide area to witness it. The headquarters of the soulers in Antrobus are at the Wheatsheaf Inn. They start there, but where they end is anybody's guess. The souling play proceeds along the accepted traditional lines until the point when the Antrobus Horse (known as the Wild Horse; **6**) makes his appearance with his driver. This is followed by a jingle, the sense of which is not always clear, but which delights the great crowds of spectators. This ditty is intended to raise money. 'The horse has a presence about him, and in the view of Mari Lwyd (**7**), hoodening, hobby horses and the like, he may have had a more significant rôle in the past' (pp.187-9, Shuel, *National Trust Guide*).

7a *(top) The Mari Lwyd at Maesteg*
7b *(bottom) At The Old House, Llangynwyd, Mid Glamorgan, the Mari Lwyd is put away until next Christmas.*

Christmas (*Nadolig*)

As in Scotland, so in Wales; Christmas was given second place to the pagan festival of the New Year. Today things have evened out somewhat. Nevertheless, I think it is true to say that the New Year celebrations and holiday do, in practice, assume a position of greater importance. Christmas tended to replace the winter solstice by substituting the birth of Christ as the underlying message of the feast. However, it is almost impossible to totally eradicate superstitious practices in areas where they have occurred from time immemorial and are deeply built into the psyche of the people. To avoid overt hostility, some degree of tact has been essential in order to allow society to participate in both the Christmas and the New Year celebrations (*Y Gwyliau*). The richer farmers in any given locality used to invite all the other farmers and cotters to a huge feast on Christmas day, which consisted of beef, goose perhaps and the usual accompaniments — no doubt the *cwrw* (beer) would flow and perhaps wine would be imbibed. At any rate we can rest assured that no matter what or how much was drunk it would not be in excess of the degree of sobriety necessary for the proper observances of Christmas. In some farms the plough, which would be laid up for the Christmas period, was put under the table in the dining room. After Christmas, parties of the men used to go about the houses where they would be hospitably entertained on *cwrw da*, 'good beer'. A charming habit was to wet the plough under the table with beer, so as not to leave it out of the celebrations — after all, what could a farmer do without his plough? This they did before touching the beer themselves. Thus the valuable services of the plough were acknowledged and the men could get on with their own imbibing.

In a part of Carmarthenshire in the 1860s, Christmas had little significance. It was neither Sunday or a work day; Trefor Owen calls it a 'colourless day' (p.28). Christmas day itself could be rather dull and it was much more exciting to look forward to the *Plygain*. *Plygain*, which was once common throughout Wales, but is now more or less confined to certain areas of the country, consisted of a gathering in the candle-lit churches, formerly at midnight, for carol singing in Welsh, performing in groups or parties. Each possesses their own book of carols, which they still guard with the utmost jealousy and prize almost above all other possessions. Today, many of the handwritten carol books are still in existence, but the whole emphasis of the night's entertainment has changed. The church is not universally in favour of the *Plygain* because the young men were using the festive occasion for drinking to excess and upsetting the religious community with rowdy behaviour. Of course the churches are no longer lit by candles as they were up to 40 or 50 years ago, but by electric light.

A good neighbour of mine took us to the *Plygain* at Llanerfyl, Powys, where the tradition remains very strong. The vicar, an excellent man, opened the proceedings of the evening and then sat quietly enjoying the wonderful quality of the Welsh voices, surely refined and softened by the moist air of the mountainous countryside. Groups of perhaps six, seven or even ten people, known as 'parties' (*partïon*) carrying their priceless family carol books and wearing their Sunday best, walked briskly and confidently to the front of the church, took their note from the organist's tuning fork and began to sing. The *Plygain* singing is always unaccompanied. The power and quality of their performance really had to be experienced to be believed. Every one of these 'parties' performed with consummate excellence and the strange and, to the outsider's ear, wild archaism of the singing made this evening one never to be forgotten. The performance lasted for about two hours. There was one solo singer, a little, frail old man who managed, after one or two attempts, to get the right note from the tuning fork. He then walked with great dignity to the central position and I felt very distressed and nervous for him, having no expectation that he could so much as make his voice heard. It was a great shock when he began to sing, to hear the tremendous strength and vitality of his voice, and his unerring correctness of notes. Everyone was totally still and, as verse followed verse, each one seemed to be more powerful and more beautifully modulated. It was a moving moment. Finally, a group of young men, all tall and dark and smartly dressed, marched vigorously up towards the pulpit where the vicar was waiting for them. They all then indulged in an amusing ritual. He told them that now they must 'sing for their supper' and sing they did, with eager anticipation of the marvellous meal that awaited them in the church hall, and which we had earlier observed being prepared as we walked from the car to the church. No labour or expense had been spared in order to make this a joyous occasion; and the flawless performances of all concerned were rewarded in the best way they could wish — by giving them an excellent supper! It was a long drive back home, but a deep sense of achievement and content filled us all. We knew we had witnessed something with an unbroken tradition behind it which made it stand apart from the worthy but essentially modern revivals of the *Plygain* that are taking place in certain areas where it has long died out, or never before been performed.

All the *Plygain* ceremonies were not as restrained and dignified as that at Llanerfyl. The performance appears to have taken place originally between three and six a.m., hence the Latin name *pulli cantio*, which means 'cockcrow'. One can imagine the long weary hours of waiting and these were occupied in a variety of ways, not always beneficial to society. This is probably why the *Plygain* got a bad name in latter years. To fill in the hours until the service, making treacle toffee was seemingly a favourite distraction; and this was also the time to decorate the dwelling houses with holly and mistletoe. Some people danced away the time accompanied by harp music and singing until the service was due to begin. Others simply took to the streets and indulged in rowdy games until morning, carrying huge homemade torches, which gave out a satisfactory light, but must have been somewhat dangerous. Verses were chanted, torches carried and cow-horns blown. In Tenby, for example, horns were blown before getting in position for the torch procession, in which the vicar was led by the young men of the town from the vicarage to the church. The torches, however, were not taken into the church but left in the porch until the service was over when they were relighted. Of course, there was no provision for lighting in the churches, services normally being held during the day. There were however special candles made called *canhwyllau Plygain* (*Plygain* candles). These were sold, and one could choose a large candle or a small one, according to one's means.

New Year (*Blwyddyn Newydd*)

The Welsh practised first-footing, as did many other peoples at New Year. It was, and is, a time to look ahead, and to look back. People look ahead to the coming year in the hope that things (including themselves) will improve and be better by the end of the year. In order to do this, they looked back into the dying year and tried to identify the chief faults and failures which made them hope for a better controlled future. There is a great deal of folklore widely associated with New Year's Eve. In my own home events were rigorously supervised by my father, a man practical by nature, but nonetheless deeply

8 New Year customs (top) Clennig, after R. Holland 1992, p.51 (bottom) Calennig, after T. M. Owen 1987, pl.6

influenced by the superstitions of his family past. A bottle of port must be at hand to offer the first person to come to the door after midnight struck. It was a sign of good luck if he was dark-haired, and he must always carry a piece of coal symbolising the rekindling of the new fire. It was always said: 'Out with the old, in with the new' and one really felt that this moment heralded a new beginning in every way: a chance to remedy faults, correct errors and determine to be better and, in my case, work harder at my studies. It was taken very seriously. Many members of the family then gathered at the house, and we all crossed hands and sang the good old Scottish tune, Auld Lang Syne. Things were not much different in Wales, although sometimes entry was denied to a house and the 'lettings in' were customs. The giving and receiving of a *Callenig* or *Clennig* (New Year's Gift) (**8**) seemingly still continues in the country to some extent. Some houses — and people — were sprinkled by local boys with fresh water from a spring, in which appropriate herbs and twigs had been soaked and in return a few pennies were given to these youngsters.

There is much more that could be recounted concerning the old New Year customs, but space is limited. I have included in the bibliography one or two further references for those who feel the subject could have been covered more fully.

Gwyl Fair y Canhwyllau (Candlemas)

This festival, held on 2 February, is in honour of the Purification of the Virgin Mary after the birth of Christ. It is a sweet and tranquil occasion. Today it has sadly fallen into wide disuse but right up to the twentieth century it was celebrated in many ways, both by church-going and by the placing of a lit candle in the windows of every house, symbolising both the religious and the secular aspects of the feast. It celebrated the safe birth of the Christ-child and the purification of his mother. It was also symbolic of the earth rising from slumber into a period of abundance and newness of life. The soil had to be tilled, the seed sown and the work of the farm or cottage was once again of prime importance with a view to a favourable spring, leading to the fullness of fruition of summer. It was therefore a portentous time, a time to ensure that all would go well with the land and those who worked it. Trefor Owen mentions a charming Wassail song of the seventeenth century which called this day *Gwyl Fair Forwyn ddechre gwanwyn*, 'the feast to mark the beginning of spring'. Owen comments that:

> In this article, it is intended to look in some detail at the distinctive way Candlemas . . . was celebrated in a particular part of Wales, central Caernarvonshire, at a specific point in time, namely the middle of the eighteenth century. My choice is governed by the evidence available which is, fortunately, sufficient to enable a fairly clear picture to be drawn of the mode of celebrating the festival at a time when it still possessed a wealth of meaning for the countryman in this part of north Wales. Much of our information about customs in late eighteenth- and early nineteenth-century Wales comes from the accounts of travellers, who sought the romantic and the picturesque, not only in scenery but in tradition, custom and living conditions generally (p.240). Candlemas carols occur (or are preserved) far less frequently than the Christmas *Plygain* carols. Among the Candlemas carols, the peculiar *carolau cadair* or 'chair carols' are very rare indeed and relate to the Caernarvon district in the second half of the eighteenth century, with a few earlier Anglesey examples . . .

There is also a collection of wassail carols (*carolau gwirod*) likewise connected with Candlemas, written down by Richard Morris of Anglesey (1703-79) (*vide* T.H. Parry-Williams, *Llawysgrif Richard Morris o Cerddi*, Cardiff 1931). Owen continues:

> The custom began, after dark on Candlemas eve, with *canu yn drws* (singing at the door). A common feature in the folk tradition throughout Wales occurring in the Mari Lwyd tradition in Glamorgan and Gwent and in the *pwnco* or question and answer in verse which was characteristic of the wedding customs of Dyfed.

When the 'carol at the door' and the proper responses were completed and access had been gained to the house the singers demanded in rhyming words that a chair should be placed in the middle of the floor. In one version after similar opening verses have been sung on entry into the house, a request is made, amongst others, that a youthful virgin be asked to sit in the chair with a six-week-old baby boy on her knee. This was obviously an imitation of the Virgin and the Christ-child. The chance of obtaining 'a virgin as pure as Mary' must have been somewhat limited. There is much more and references are given to the publications relating to this ritual. We should recognise firstly that there must have been regional variations and secondly that for some centuries after the Reformation the cult of the virgin was regarded with disapprobation. The highlight of the *Gwyl Fair* festival occurred when the final stanza of one of the 'chair carols' asks that the party should be led to the corner of the room in order to partake of the beer. For a similar end to a festival see *Plygain*.

When we are considering the history of Welsh tradition we must remember what an enormous impact the Reformation must have had on the ancient traditions. The old religion of Catholicism officially gave way to Protestantism, which frowned upon many of the old Catholic-based customs, of which *Gwyl Fair* was one. It is not easy to rob people of a cherished past, with all its traditions; but it is necessary in such harsh times of religious persecution to let the old ways continue in secret. This can, of course, gradually erode them, as those who knew and valued them disappear. It is my belief that much that did survive was probably to some extent due to the shepherds who, after long hours on the hills, and facing a rough and lengthy walk back to their homes, lightened the labours by telling the old tales and stories which had comforted or frightened them in childhood and reciting the old, familiar verses, which they had been taught orally in their early years. In my experiences with shepherds from the Scottish Highlands I have always been amazed, not only by their deep knowledge of the local traditions, but of their wider understanding of the great poets and writers. The same, I believe, can be applied to Wales, although we have to remind ourselves that we are today probably witnessing the very end of these archaic customs and beliefs. Nevertheless, an astonishing amount of tradition — and the people's pleasure in it — is still with us and its power in surviving changes of a major political, religious and economic nature testify to this.

May Day (*Calan Mai*)

This is sometimes abbreviated to *Clamme*. In keeping with all Celtic festivals the feast or the celebrations began on the eve of the day. On May Day Eve, which was an *ysbrydnos*, one of the three 'spirit nights', it was believed that, as in midsummer and on Hallowe'en, the ghosts of the dead manifested themselves and haunted the countryside and that various supernatural forces were abroad. As with the other major Celtic festivals, bonfires used to be lit on May Day Eve. This pertained more to South than to North Wales, and persisted into the nineteenth century. Lewis Morris (*vide* Trefor Owen, p.97) gives such an important account of this practice, and it contains so many elements which really belong to ancient Celtic religion, that I feel it is worth quoting in full:

> The fire was done in this way; nine men would turn their pockets inside out and see that every piece of money and all metals were off their persons. Then the men went into the nearest woods, and collected sticks of nine different kinds of trees. These were carried to the spot where the fire had to be built. There a circle was cut in the sod and the sticks were set crosswise. All around the circle the people stood and watched the proceedings. One of the men would then take two bits of oak, and rub them together until a full flame was kindled. This was applied to the sticks, and soon a large fire was made. Sometimes two fires were set up side by side. These fires, whether one or two, were called *coelcerth* or bonfire. Round cakes of oatmeal and bran meal were split in four and placed in a small flour-bag, and everybody present had to pick out a portion. The last bit in the bag fell to the lot of the bag-holder. Each person who chanced to pick up a piece of bran-meal cake was compelled to leap three times over the flames, or to run thrice between the two fires, by which means the people thought they were sure of a plentiful harvest. Shouts and screams of those who had to face the ordeal could be heard ever so far, and those who chanced to pick up the oatmeal portions sang and danced and clapped their hands in approval, as the holders of the brown bits leaped three times over the flames, or ran three times between the two fires. As a rule, no danger attended these celebrations, but occasionally somebody's clothes caught fire, which was quickly put out . . . I have also heard my grandfather say that in times gone by the people would throw a calf in the fire when there was any disease among the herds. The same would be done with a sheep if there was anything the matter with the flock. I can remember myself

> seeing cattle being driven between the two fires to 'stop the disease spreading'. When in later times it was not considered humane to drive the cattle between the fires, the herdsmen were accustomed to force the animals over the wood ashes to protect them against various ailments. People carried the ashes left after these fires to their homes, and a charred brand was not only effectual against pestilence, but magical in its use. A few of the ashes placed in a person's shoes protected the wearer from any great sorrow or woe.

Augury was also practised on May Day Eve. Lewis Morris records an Anglesey form of the ceremony, *Swper nos Glanmai* (supper on May Day Eve). He also refers to the custom of 'Playing the Straw Man' — *gware gêr gwellt* — but gives no further details. It seems to echo in a more innocent fashion the descriptions of the great straw images of men, filled with living sacrifices, and offered to the gods in Gaul (Diodorus Siculus, *Hist.* V. 32; Kendrick, *The Druids*, p.121-2).

May Day was the first day of summer, *Calan Mai*. It used to be known as *Calan Haf*, 'the summer calend'. Although it was in late autumn, the other important, ancient festival was known as *Calan Gaeaf*, 'the winter calend' (1 November), which was also the Celtic New Year. These are the two most important of the ancient *ysbryd nosau* ('spirit nights') and go right back to the time when the Celtic year was divided into two major portions. The other calendar festivals are secondary accretions which became equally popular, but perhaps of less significance. The maypole (*cangen haf*) was the focal point for many of the archaic survivals which are still vestigially recognised at the present time, although their basic significance has inevitably changed. An interesting line about the maypole celebrating the festival occurs in one of the poems of the great medieval poet, Dafydd Benfras (1230-60). He was a court poet and soldier living in dark and difficult times; he was killed in battle and apparently buried at Llangadog in Carmarthenshire. He describes, in Welsh, the taking of a birch tree from his own locality, over the hills to Llanidloes and to its being set up in the market place to celebrate *Calan Mai*. The birch tree was the most popular tree for use as the maypole. Its foliage is at its most beautiful then, and when stripped from the trunk of the tree, would no doubt be used to adorn houses and other buildings. Although the latter-day birch was felled for the May celebrations, it is not unlikely that originally the celebrations may have taken place about a living tree and it has been commented that there is a close association of the birch with love by many Welsh poets. The dance around the maypole was sometimes accompanied by the music of the pipes, and the maypole custom called *codi'r fedwen* (raising the birch) in the South; in the North *y gangen haf* (the summer branch). Dancing round the maypoles was popular and there was virtually no end to the various kinds of activity with which this special day was filled. The day progressed with all kinds of communal ploys: mask-wearing, ridiculous clothing, merry-making, feasting and dancing in front of farmhouses. Householders were asked for money and the boys would dance, and so things continued all day. A good deal has been written about the May dancing, and some further reading suggestions are made in the bibliography.

It was a fine time for flowers, wild and cultivated (**9**), which the people used to gather and give as posies to their girlfriends or to the heads of households. On the morning of May Day, people went to the fields and meadows to collect cowslips and then went home and decorated the house outside; the door, the windows, the gate and the path were all strewn with flowers; well-heads were also decorated. Other plants such as trees could be used, according to what was available in any given locality. In Radnor rowan and birch branches (*cangen haf*) were gathered, and the birch tree was, as we have seen, frequently used for the maypole. May Day was begun with the singing of *carolau Mai*, or *carolau haf* (May or summer carols), and *canu haf*, summer singing. The singers, on visiting a family on a May morning, saluted them on the appearance of summer and the high expectation of the season. Many summer carols seem to have been written by clergymen, and were serious rather than flippant in character. Sometimes they help to clarify what really happened at these celebrations. We are not sure when the May Day celebrations originated, but there is no doubt of their great popularity.

9 Welsh Poppy. 'In rocky woods and shady places, in the hilly districts of western Europe from Spain to Ireland, Wales and the western counties of England.' G. Bentham and J.D. Hooker, 1924 (1945), p.20, fig.41

There was a great variety of customs, all of which were competitive: indeed, little in the way of customs has survived unless they are competitive, such as *Gwyl fair y gwirodau*, one of several feasts created for the Virgin. There was also a great deal of carol-singing and drinking of alcohol (T. Gwynn Jones *et al.*, p.100).

The carols that were sung were traditional carols based on the life of the Virgin Mary. There was also the custom of walking round or 'making rounds' of a fire. The *gwyl mabsant*, saint's day, was kept in every parish.

Games were played and there were competitions of every kind and it attracted great numbers of people. Overnight accommodation was scarce and people had to provide makeshift bedding on the floor. This custom caused the beds to be known as *gwely gwyl mabsant*. The festivals were usually held on Sundays but often began the day before, and carried on until the following Tuesday! There was every kind of contest, such as cock-fighting, football, hurling, wrestling, leaping and running. In the football (*pêl-droed*), the team would consist of men from two different parishes, in opposition to each other, and the ones who lost the match had to provide the successful team with beer. In some places, relics of the saints were carried. In the eighteenth century certain churchmen attempted to terminate these riotous meetings or to move them to weekdays. There were many such meetings; drunkenness and aggressive behaviour seem to have been the order of the day at these eighteenth-century gatherings.

The *Mari Lwyd* (Grey Mary)

The Christmas season was of lesser importance in Wales than the festivities of the New Year. This was also the case in Scotland, right down to the middle of the twentieth century, in many places. Customs observed in this season include *Calan Gaeaf*, (the Calends of winter), and *gwyl mabsant* (festival of the patron saint). The *Plygain* we have already mentioned. Some of the Christmas legends were similar to those of Gaelic Scotland, but several are quite different and of interest. The plant rosemary and the sacred thorn that allegedly sprang from a living branch of thorn brought from the Holy Land by Joseph of Arimathea as his staff, allegedly planted at Glastonbury in the first century AD, is still believed to have survived. Cuttings were taken from it, according to tradition, to ensure its continuance down the long centuries. True or not, many people visit Glastonbury at this season to see the wondrous tree in bloom, as I myself have done. There is a tradition that a Welshman made the pilgrimage and took a cutting from the thorn, which grew into a fine tree.

Ever popular was the *Mari Lwyd*. This extraordinary 'hobby horse' consisted of the skull of a horse which was buried for some time in a pit lined with quicklime or in the ground to excarnate the head (*see* **7**). The lower jaw was fitted up with springs which made the mouth shut with a loud clap as it was operated by the one who was carrying it. A substantial pole, some 5ft in length, was fixed into the horse's skull and a pure white sheet was draped over it to give the impression of the animal's body. The skull was decorated with different coloured ribbons and coloured glass was used for the eyes. Ears made of remnants of black cloth were sewn onto the white sheet, and the result was extremely impressive. The man whose job it was to carry the horse got under the sheet, held the pole and operated the lower jaw by means of a wooden handle, making it 'snap' in an alarming manner. Reins with bells were attached to the head and these were held by the leader of the troupe who also carried the stick for the purpose of knocking on doors during the performance. Verses were chanted and people gave presents or asked the horse in. A lot of fun and joking took place, but the overall ritual was fairly rigid, although it allowed for some variation in detail. This was a Glamorgan custom, and it survived perhaps longer than any other of the 'horsings' which were once common more widely in Wales. The name of the horse differed from place to place and records or folk memory show that it was a very popular festival and could sometimes last for several days.

The party which accompanied the Glamorgan horse consisted of the horse itself, the Leader who held the reins, then the 'sergeant', the 'merry man' and 'Punch and Judy'. Merry Man sometimes played the fiddle and Punch and Judy had blackened faces and they would all be dressed up in colourful clothes with sashes about their waists. The entire group or party went round the whole neighbourhood and engaged in a battle of wits with each household by chanting extempore verse which had to be replied to by a wittier composition from inside the house. When the Mari Lwyd was permitted to go into a house, the horse apparently made for the women and pretended to bite them, neighed at them, butted into them and blew on them. When the horse left the house, after much rumbustious and rather risqué play, the Leader would say, in Welsh, 'We wish you joy to live a new year; as long as the man tinkles his bell, may every day get better.' The origin of this festival is not clear; many suggestions have been made but none of them seem to offer a really satisfactory solution. Such horsings were known at one time throughout Wales and also in Cheshire, where the Antrobus Horse consists of a real horse's head painted 'shiny black' and likewise mounted on a pole. (Shuel p.179)(*see* **6**). Two other such horse festivals are the famed Padstow horse of Cornwall, which performs on 1 May, as does the equally popular Minehead horse of Somerset. These festivals are still in full swing. In Wales, as elsewhere, horses' heads were buried under the foundations of the front doors of houses, as a protection against evil spirits, under the hearth and sometimes one on either side of the chimney-breast. One cannot regard these widespread folk practices as signs of horse-worship — although this certainly was the case at an earlier period in the British Isles, as archaeology attests — but they were indubitably the focus of superstition. See, for example, the belief in water-horses known as *ceffylau dwr* in Wales and those known as *each uisge* in the Scottish Highlands.

4 Medieval references to archaic Welsh folklore

Arthur

Arthur, the Once and Future King (*Rex quondam Rex que futurus*), is, has been, and in all probability will remain, an enigma. King Arthur from earliest records, from place-names (*see* **2**), and from folklore and literary sources has occupied the thoughts and time of countless people, both academic and lay; all have succumbed to the fascination of the question: 'Who was Arthur?' Did he ever exist? If so, was he a historical figure, and are there reliable records from which we may trace something of his *Vita*? He is known throughout the Celtic countries; his name occurs in connection with dramatic field monuments such as tumuli, standing stone circles, graves and so on — although it is said that the grave of Arthur will never be known. That, of course, would not be surprising, as he was alleged not to have died, but to have been transported to the sacred island of Avalon, possibly a site near Glastonbury (Ynys Wydrin), Somerset, which is much concerned with his legend.

There are, of course, other stories of his 'demise'. In Wales there is a legend that Arthur did not die. He and his warriors allegedly lie sleeping in a cave on Snowdon (Yr Wyddfa), fully armed, their weapons beside them, waiting until they are roused by the call to save Britain from disaster. This is one of many beliefs that have accrued round the shadowy folk hero whom we call Arthur, who remains an enigmatic character — a figure of folklore and a focus for endless academic speculation. It is sufficient to say that the name of King Arthur has attained to great heights of popularity in the British Isles, as in Europe, dating in written records to the medieval period and down to the present day, where the controversy still rages.

As we have seen, Arthur represents the longed-for magical protector of his people, the one who will come again and save them from their enemies, who in the earliest written records were the Saxons. But who was he, and when did he really live? Or was he always a figure of legend, folklore and perhaps mythology? Strangely, in spite of all the scholarly research that has been carried out, this is still a very difficult question to answer. Perhaps scholars generally believe that an Arthur, a Dark Age leader of the British against the Saxons did exist; but our historical data are hardly prolific.

It seems perhaps more likely that the legend of King Arthur began like that of so many folk heroes, as a Celtic deity of an all-purpose type — warrior, protector, magic-worker, leader of raids and exploits into the Otherworld, a typical god of the people, a British Teutates (*vide* Ross, *Druids* p.51) In this way the story of Arthur of mythology and oral tradition would be likely to find its way into the legend of an historical leader of the same name — perhaps even himself named after the deity-cum-folk-hero in the first place. Here we are primarily concerned with the manifestations of Arthur in Welsh literature as an archaic figure around whom many myths and folklore have evolved.

Arthur as a god

Is there any evidence for a deity of this type in Celtic mythology? The answer must be in the affirmative, although the actual evidence is limited. It is possible, from the Gaulish evidence, to glimpse what may be a divine predecessor for the 'historical' Arthur. The name — in Latin Arturius, in British Artorius — , has its roots in the word *art*, 'bear' (old Celtic *Artos*, 'bear' from *arta*). This would seem to be a pan-Celtic word and Arthur is possibly in origin a universal Celtic god-type. The bear was an important cult animal throughout the Celtic world where it was indigenous. In early Irish, *art* means 'bear', 'warrior', 'god'. This is easy to understand. The bear is the only animal to walk on two legs. This gives him the appearance of a great, shaggy warrior; it is matched by his feared ferocity. Celtic warriors used to wear animal skins in battle and for warmth and the Celts also buried dead warriors in animal pelts.

The Celts feared more than anything the prospect of the heavens falling upon the earth. A great bear rearing up to strike down upon a human being must have been akin to this catastrophe. A sculpture from Linsdorf, Haut-Rhin — possibly dating to the heyday of early Celtic culture and art — takes the form of a great, menacing, fanged bear, pressing down with his murderous claws on the severed heads of two warriors (**10**). Images of bears occur widely in Europe. More importantly, both a bear god and an ursine goddess are figured and invoked in Europe in the early Roman period. A small bronze head of a bear was recently excavated from road-metal in the Gaulish hill fort Camp Celtique de la Bure, near Saint-Dié, Vosges (**11**). A terracotta image of a bear from Altbachtal, near Trier, Rheinland-Pfalz and a rock-cut inscription, *ARTIONI BIBER*, near Bollendorf, on the left bank of the river Sauer, in Germany, a short distance upstream from Echternach, Luxembourg, testify to the presence of this cult among the Treveri. A bronze group from Muri is preserved in the nearby museum of Berne, Switzerland. A stately seated goddess holds out fruits to a female bear (**12**) which emerges amiably from a wood — is this herself in ursine form? The

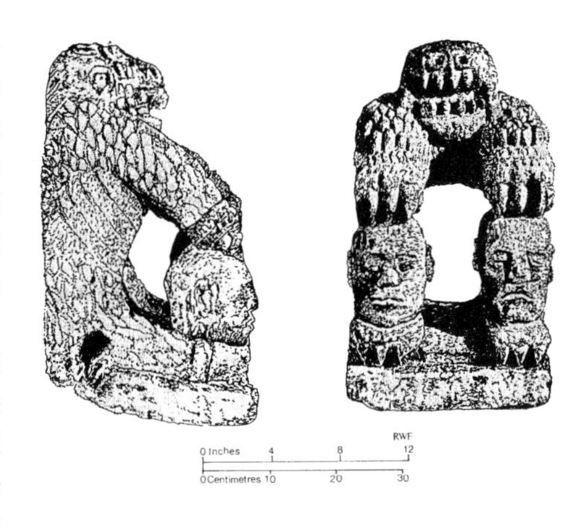

10 The Monster, Linsdorf, Haut-Rhin, France

name *ARTAIOS* (*MERCVRIO AVG. ARTAIO*) occurs on an altar, now lost, from near Beaucroissant, Isère (**13**). It has been suggested that here the god was invoked as the deity who protects travellers (from bears?).

A medieval Rhenish legend indicates an ancient cult of the bear in connection with sacred sources. There are other, stone representations of bears from Gallo-Roman sites. A bear-goddess, Andarta, meaning 'extremely powerful bear', was invoked at Dea Augusta, Die, Drôme. Welsh *arthgen* means 'descended from the bear god'; Irish *artigan* is 'son of the bear'. Bears are amongst several stone figures of probable Iron Age date. These were found in what was obviously a shrine for some bear cult when repair work was being carried out in the graveyard of the Cathedral on Cathedral Hill, Armagh City, Northern Ireland. Raftery (p.185) mentions these bears and says: 'It is thus possible that a bear cult existed in the Armagh region . . . ' There is another word for 'bear' in Ireland which is more common than *art*. This is *math*, an archaic word which was replaced in early Middle Irish by *mathgamain*, 'bear', Latin *ursus*. There is an Irish Druid whose name is Mathgen, 'born of a bear'; and one wonders about the enchanter Math in the *Mabinogion* of Wales. In early Irish, *mathmarcóir* means 'augur'; *mathmarc* is used in Medieval texts for 'soothsayer'.

Fionn MacCumhaill figures as Ffin fab Koel (*Trioedd Ynys Prydein*, '*TYP*', lxxxii and Bartrum p.222): Edyrn ap Gwythno Garanhir, the man who went to run with the wind when a huge fleet came to carry off the wife of Ffin ap Coel by violence. Evidently Fionn MacCumhaill the Irish hero is meant; the reference is interesting as possible evidence for the merging of characters from Irish stories into Welsh narrative of which there are further instances: see *TYP* p.400.

It is useful to now consider some other points of similarity between the two main sources of Celtic mythology, Welsh and Irish, which have some bearing on the Arthur question, a problem which still occupies scholars today. As Proinsias McCana neatly puts it: 'The original Arthur may well have been a historical character, but the King Arthur of medieval romance, and his knightly entourage, are much larger than life, and share many of the mythological traits of the Irish Fionn MacCumhaill and his Fianna.'

11 Bronze head of Bear from le Camp Celtique de la Bure, Saint-Dié, Vosges, France

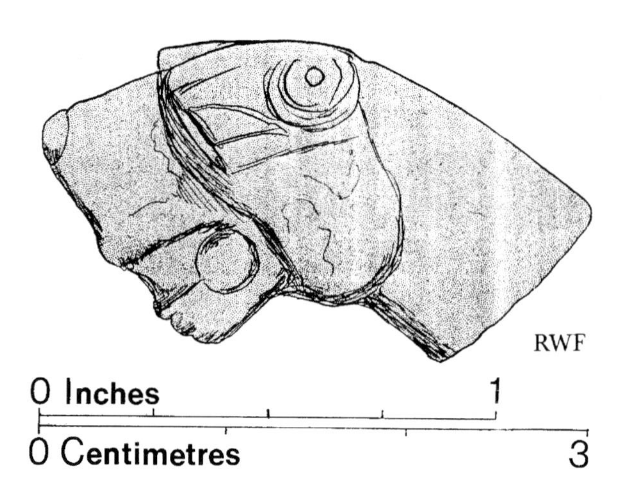

Emhain Abhlach, 'Emhain of the apple-trees', an Irish Otherworld — which the literature identifies with the beautiful island of Arran in the Firth of Clyde, off the south-west coast of Scotland — finds a close parallel in Arthur's Avalon, 'place of apples', the gentle Otherworld to which he is borne after his 'fatal' wounding. According to tradition, of course, he did not really die, but lies sleeping, waiting for the time when his people need him most urgently, when he will come and save them. Of particular interest is the fact that this same legend is attached to Fionn MacCumhaill and his warriors, and like the Arthur belief, there are several sites, usually caves, in which he is said to be resting.

Many place-names in Ireland and Britain commemorate both Fionn and Arthur (*see* **2**). Their legends left their impression on the landscape; they were both familiar with the Wilderness.

The Divine Protector

Both Fionn and Arthur are often portrayed as ageing leaders. Arthur is not always so depicted, as we shall see. The earliest appearances of Arthur make him a very close parallel to Fionn, as does his hypothetical divinity. Both defend their countries against foreign enemies, both have elevated positions. In the ninth century, Nennius refers to Arthur as *Dux Bellorum*, a close parallel to Fionn's title, *Righfhéinnidh*. Both Fionn and Arthur fight and vanquish fierce monsters and supernatural creatures. Both invade the Otherworld and bring away treasure; both are associated with magical cauldrons; both are hunters.

Perhaps the most interesting parallel is the fact that they are each pursuers of metamorphosed boars. Moreover, Twrch Trwyth, a magical, enchanted boar, originally a king, is known in Ireland as Orc Tréith. Arthur hunts this

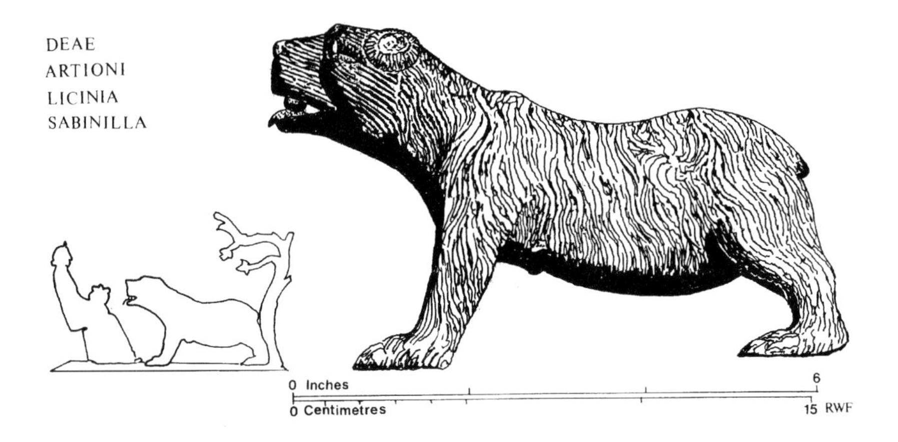

12 DEAE ARTIONI LICINIA SABINILLA, Muri, Switzerland

creature through parts of Ireland, Cornwall and south Wales. Many legends about this great boar must have been current in both countries. Fionn hunts numerous magical pigs, some of which are transformed from human shape, all of which retain their human wisdom and understanding. Legends about both Fionn and Arthur and their exploits circulated in the oral tradition for centuries, and actually received the approval of the literati — the Arthurian legend from the twelfth century, the Fionn cycle from the eighteenth century.

The Sword Excalibur

This popular name for Arthur's sword is derived from the name *Calibernus* used by Geoffrey of Monmouth. The Welsh name is *Caledfwlch.* In the medieval story of Culhwch and Olwen, it is named as one of Arthur's most precious possessions; it is used by Llenlleawg Wyddel to kill Diwrnach Wyddel and his men. The weapon is described in the Welsh versions of *Historia Regum Britanniae* as the finest sword ever made in Ynys Afallach (the Island of Afallon). It is the weapon Arthur brandishes when he fights the great giant on Mont Saint Michel (Mynydd Mihangel).

Culhwch ac Olwen is the earliest of the Welsh prose tales. It may have been committed to writing as early as the eleventh century, after centuries of circulation in the oral tradition of Britain. It is a complex story, but it is the folkloric and mythological elements that concern us here. In outline, Olwen is the giant Ysbadaddern's daughter and in order to prevent her marriage, her father puts many virtually impossible tasks to Culhwch before he will agree to his marriage with his daughter. It was prophesied that her father would meet his death when she became a bride.

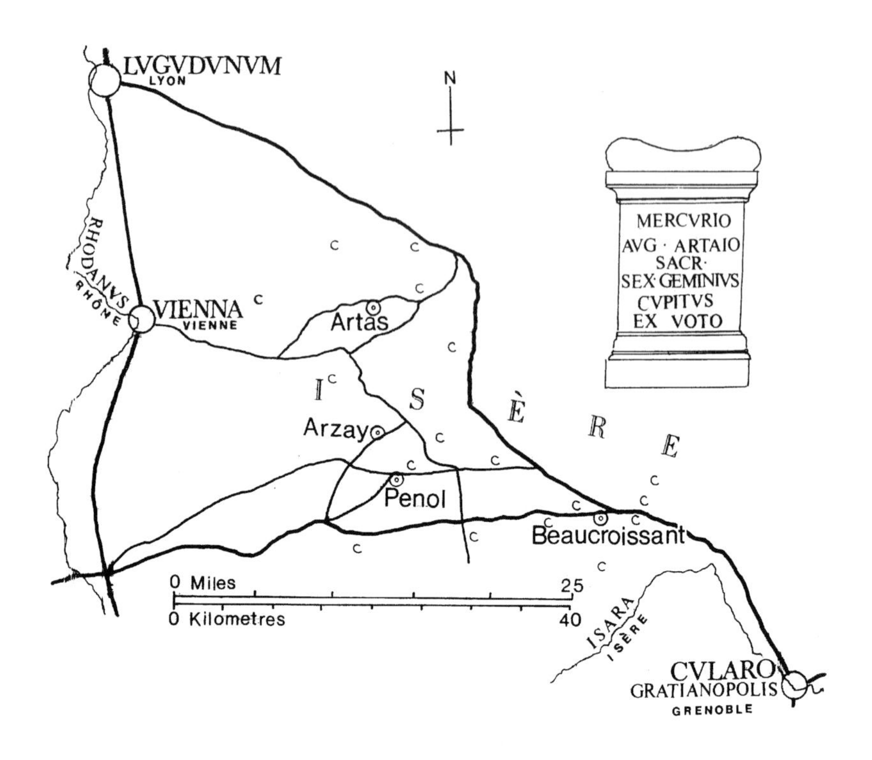

13 Map showing the location of Beaucroissant, Isère, France, the site of the lost altar (inset); the letter C refers to châteaux

Perhaps one of the most interesting features of the story is the character of Arthur. He is described as *Penteyrnedd yr Ynys hon*, 'chief of the princes of this island'. This compares well with Fionn's regal title of *Righ Fhéinnidh*, 'the King of the Fian'. Arthur has the same power over people; he can even command the animals. Monsters fall by his hand; prisoners are taken and released at his command. When he goes to Ireland the saints go to him to ask for his protection. Oisín, Fionn's son, enjoys a gracious relationship with St Patrick and his clerics. The magic, enchanted boar, Twrch Trwyth, whom they must hunt, and his followers, also transformed humans, do not however accede to his demands.

The popular concept of Arthur was that of a protector of the land, a protagonist of monsters and hags, and a benefactor of prisoners. Arthur traditionally fought with many powerful opponents on Welsh hilltops, and here again we may draw close parallels with Fionn of Irish tradition. Arthur adjudicates in the quarrel between Gwyn ap Nudd (Fionn's closest linguistic counterpart in Welsh mythology), just as Fionn does with the Tuatha Dé

Danann. 'Whatever Arthur's ultimate origins may be, in early literature he belongs, like Fionn, to the realm of mythology rather than to that of history.' (Bromwich, *Culhwch* p.xxix)

Arthur is associated with another magical pig-hunt (*vide TYP* p.48). It is part of the Triad known as The Three Powerful Swineherds of the Island of Britain. It is of considerable importance in view of the eminent place given to swine and swineherds in the folklore and mythology of the Celts in general and the remarkable association of swineherds with Druids. Both the Welsh text and the translation are given in *TYP* p.45ff. It is too long and detailed to include in this section but it is sufficient to say that the hunt for the transformed pigs takes place on land and sea and Henwen ('the Old White One'), who is pregnant, has to keep stopping in order to bring forth. The contents of her womb are most remarkable. In Maes Gwynedd, in Gwent, she gave birth to a grain of wheat and a bee, but her pregnancy was not over. Off she went to Llonion in Pembroke and there gave birth to a wolf-cub and a young eagle. She ran away again and went to Llanfair-yn-Arfon, Caernarvon, where she gave birth to a kitten; the enchanter and magical swineherd Coll, son of Collfrewi, who was looking after the pigs, threw it from the rock into the sea and the sons of Palug found it and reared it in Anglesey (Môn), which did them no good.

That was the origin of Palug's Cat which was to become One of the Three Great Oppressions of Môn, which were reared on the island. Cath Palug (**14**) belongs to Celtic mythology and folklore, and is related to a whole series of monster cats which figure in Irish tradition. It seems that the cat has never been popular with the Celts — here I depart from the norm, having 16 gentle and much-loved felines! The alleged unpopularity may be due to its supposed association with the malevolent Otherworld and the fact that it figures as a companion of witches and other baleful beings. The most fascinating item of information about Cath Palug is that she was known in French Arthurian romance as le Capalu (late twelfth- and thirteenth-century). Cath Palug was seemingly killed by Cai in Britain, but French Arthurian tradition has a different version of the tale. There she fights with Arthur, and kills him. One passage says: 'The French have made a poem about him, that King Arthur was pushed by Capalu into the bog; then the cat killed him in battle. It then passed over to England and was not slow to conquer. It then wore the crown of the land and was the lord of the country.' (Freymond, pp.332-3). This is a very odd story. The French seemingly took Cath Palug to mean 'bog cat'. Capalu was, apparently, a man transformed into feline shape.

Cath Palug keeps the character of a water monster in the medieval French sources. In the Welsh Triad she is a strong swimmer. In the Irish tradition the monster cats are called *murchat*, 'sea-cats'. The French *Estoire de Merlin* depicts Arthur fighting a battle with a monster cat near a lake. The place where he

14 *Cath Palug*

fought and overcame the cat has been known since the fourteenth century as Mont du Chat Artus. Fionn likewise battled with a monster cat, Cat Neimhe, in Dublin. *Neimhe* actually means 'poisonous' so this would translate better as 'Venomous Cat'.

Another French variant of the Cath Palug legend tells how Capalu carried Arthur away to Avalon. It may be that the tradition of Arthur's death by Capalu is an archaic one and may have existed in Welsh sources at a very early period. Or again it may have survived and been circulated in Breton lore. If Capalu (and Cath Palug) was a man or a deity either transformed into an animal or having powers of becoming an animal, in this case a cat, it would fit in well with Arthur's fabled exploits against other mythical animals such as Twrch Trwydd and his likewise enchanted companions. In an interesting note by Bromwich (*TYP* 485) it is stated that the herb 'silverweed' is called in Welsh *Palf y Gath Palug*, 'Cath Palug's paw'. The name seems apposite here. We may note that in the Hebrides silverweed, *brisgein* (wild tansy), was much prized. In a note accompanying a verse about the properties of the plant, the following information is given in Carmichael's *Carmina Gadelica*, 419: 'The root was much used throughout the Highlands and Islands before the potato was introduced. It was cultivated and so grew to a considerable size. As certain places are noted for the cultivation of the potato, so certain places are noted for the cultivation of silverweed.' It was dug up: compare Welsh *palu* 'to dig'. Another monster cat is mentioned specifically in the book of Taliesin: 'The speckled cat will make havoc with its enemies, from the ford of Taradyr to Porth Wygyr in Môn.' This could well be a reference to Cath Palug.

Nearly everyone has heard of King Arthur and his Knights of the Round Table, and Arthur's ultimate rôle as the saviour of his people. This 'cycle' of tales — known as the Matter of Britain — has long passed from the literary tradition to the realms of folklore (where it no doubt began, far back in the mists of ancient Celtic mythology). I have not traced more than the outline of the stories of Arthurian characters as they appear from Welsh folklore, especially in place-names. The popularity of these tales has not lessened as the endless appearance of books, articles and lectures, television plays and documentaries of various kinds demonstrates. And to show that the topic is not peculiarly Welsh, or even British — in popularity, if not in origin — there is a current series of books including such titles as *Arthur of the Welsh* and *Arthur of the English. Arthur of the French* would be an important addition to this series, and *Arthur of the Scots* must surely be included as so much Arthurian legend is focused on North Britain and the Border lands. Edinburgh has Arthur's Seat as an impressive 'backdrop' to a fine city, crowned by an Iron Age hillfort, and many other Arthurian place-names with attendant legends. Germany too has its full quota of Arthurian tradition and a book in this series has been devoted to that country. The English, of course, have their own Arthur with his Round Table, allegedly found at Winchester in Hampshire. Cornwall and Brittany likewise are rich in traces of the legendary Arthur.

The fascination of Arthurian tales is endless, timeless, and the old gods of a pre-Arthurian period haunt the countryside of Europe side by side with these other gigantic figures of Celtic mythology. I can but guide the reader to libraries and bookshops in my own, very brief bibliography and hope that their journeys through the countryside of Wales and Europe may be made more rewarding by a perusal of some of these Arthurian volumes. Meanwhile I have limited my own interest in the subject to the brief comments relating to field monuments and recounted a few of the legends in which Arthurian characters play some distinctive rôle.

Arthur's impact on the landscape

As a leading folk hero, whose exploits in the dim past where history and mythology blend, King Arthur the Once and Future King, the legendary saviour of his people, whose grave will never be found, has left more than folk-tales as his memorial. The landscape of Wales — and indeed, as befits an international figure, a large part of the British Isles and Europe — is studded with prehistoric monuments bearing his name (**2, 15**). Usually there is a local legend as to why the monument was so named and frequently the accompanying answer to the question is an exciting and dramatic story. Books upon books are written about King Arthur and his heroic Knights and indeed one wonders whether there is anything else to be said about him. The truth is, his story is ever-expanding and newly-discovered archaeological sites can often suggest some association with him.

Wales boasts many monuments and we may perhaps begin by looking at Arthur's Stone, or *Maen Ceti* in its Welsh form, which is situated at Reynoldston in Gower (3 in figure **2**). This consists of a Neolithic chambered cairn which takes us back to the fourth or third millennia BC. It is a remarkable monument.

Comprising a huge boulder, known as *Maen* in Welsh, it is balanced precariously on a few small slabs of stone which stand upright. It is in a dramatic position and as it was obviously intended that this monument should be created, it is suggested by archaeologists that the huge boulder might have been transported here from another site. Many people do not realise how mobile the society of the Neolithic and Bronze Ages was, and how innovating. We have simply to look at the most dramatic of all stone circles, that at Stonehenge, to realise the enormous amount of labour, organisation and mathematical knowledge that must have gone into transporting huge stone slabs, perhaps from great distances, to create the universally revered monument. To return to Arthur's Stone, although it is designated as a Neolithic monument, it does not fit into any categories of such sites and it is questionable whether it is of Neolithic date. The huge capstone, which is a natural boulder of vast proportions, is of local conglomerate rock, and is believed to have weighed some 35 tons when it was intact. Part has fractured, and that now lies in three parts to the west of the monument. The base of the boulder rests on the original ground surface. There are nine uprights remaining in position but the boulder is only supported by four of these. It is not certain whether a tomb exists, but there are two squarish compartments adjacent to each other. There is no certainty as to where the entrance lies. Of interest, perhaps, is that in the westerly direction there is a large Bronze Age circular cairn.

Maen Ceti is the subject of one of the numerous triads of early Britain (*vide* Bromwich, *Trioedd Ynys Prydein*). Compare Coetan Arthur (Arthur's Quoit), St Davids (**15**).

Arthur is not only associated with field monuments of different periods but with static features in the landscape such as caves, many of which are believed to harbour treasure. There is an important cave called *Ogof Arthur*, 'Arthur's Cave', which is situated in the southern side of Mynydd y Cnwc (cf. Gaelic *cnoc*, 'mound' or 'low hill'). This is within the parish of Llangwyfan on the south-west coast of Anglesey. The foot of Mynydd y Cnwc is close to the sea where the tide washes in and the mouth of the cave is completely closed by sea water at high tide. However, the cave, which is very large, has an air-hole in the side of the mountain. It is supposed to measure a mile in length. The man who reported to the *Brython* for 1859, p.158, mentions a local tradition that the great cave contained rich treasures and that it afforded Arthur shelter for a short time during his wars with the Goidels (Gaels; *Gwyddelod*). Moreover, he describes a cromlech on the top of the hill around which there was a circle of stones, within which it is reputed and widely believed that an iron chest full of ancient gold lies buried. Various attempts have been made by local people to dig it up but they have always been prevented by evil portents. So here we find that the guardians of the treasure are in fact supernatural

15 Coetan Arthur, St Davids, Pembrokeshire

forces, as is often the case, and especially in connection with Dinas Emrys. (See further list of monuments and landscape features with the accompanying map (*see* **2**).)

Merlin (*Myrddin*)

Merlin of Wales was an immensely popular figure in Welsh literature and legend. He was regarded in the Middle Ages primarily as a man of magic capable of performing virtually impossible feats and influencing the outcome of events in a way salutary to his own people. In his rôle as prophet he became famous but by no means all his prophecies were fulfilled, unlike those of the Brahan Seer of Scottish Gaelic fame. *His* many prophecies, no matter how incredible they may have seemed when he made them, have all come true — apart from one, which is likely to do so in the future (*vide* Ross, *Folklore of the Scottish Highlands*). Prophecy was closely associated with madness in early Celtic society and those who had the *awen* ('inspiration') on them became to all appearances as one possessed, which in a sense was true. Prophecy was a kind of magic, a 'divine' inspiration, when the one possessing the gift would suddenly go into a trance-state, and thereby be enabled to see clearly future events which were often of a distressing or disastrous nature. Societies universally have had their great prophets and we have only to turn to the New Testament and the life of Christ to witness the fact that his prophetic powers were one of the most extraordinary of his many abilities. However, seeing in detail future events was a highly-developed skill amongst the

Celts and the subject of much literature and folklore. As was common widely over the Celtic world, as in other places, the person possessing such powers was not by any means always at ease with them, especially when dreadful events involved their own families and neighbours. Many would have given a great deal to be freed of the gift.

We may begin our consideration of Welsh prophecy and its most famed prophet, the renowned Merlin or Myrddin in Welsh, by noting that Ireland likewise had a renowned prophet, Suibhne Geilt. His utterances while in a trance state were strange and, to one unfamiliar with this phenomenon, bordered on madness. Merlin of Wales did indeed become a kind of madman, taking to the great forests of Celidon (Caledonia) and living like an animal — and, according to some, possessing certain animal features such as deer antlers. According to some sources he did not grow antlers but rode upon a deer which was deeply bonded with him. It is useful to note here that much Welsh folklore concerning Arthur and his advisers and retinue is closely linked to Scotland as well as being deeply embedded in the tradition of Wales. Merlin has another name apart from *Myrddin Wyllt* ('Wild Merlin'); this is Lailoken, Welsh *Llallogen* ('the honoured one').

He was an important character in medieval Welsh literature and his fame spread widely in Europe. The renowned medieval scholar, Geoffrey of Monmouth, wrote the Life (*Vita*) of the prophet in poetic form known as the *Vita Merlini*, in the twelfth century. Like Arthur, many places and archaeological features which were associated with Merlin are also associated with his name and he is one of the best-known of the medieval Welsh heroic characters. There is a traditional story that Merlin was the son of an unmarried woman who had slept but once with his father in order to procreate a pure child. The reason for this was seemingly as follows: the tyrant Vortigern (Welsh Gwrtheyrn) wished to construct a fortress but he could never get further than the foundations, clearly because some supernatural force was interfering with the building. This is a widespread folk motif. Vortigern consulted a wise man who told him that his stronghold would never be built unless these unstable foundations were first sprinkled with the blood of the pure child who had already been born, according to prophecy. Gwrtheyrn consulted his Druids on this matter and they told him that the fortress must be sprinkled with the blood of a child who had no father. Merlin's mother was found and said that she had never known a man except on one occasion and that union had resulted in the birth of the 'wonder child' Merlin/Myrddin. This satisfied Gwrtheyrn and his Druids, and the boy was taken to the stronghold. When the child realised what his fate was to be he asked for 'wise men' or Druids to be brought to him and questioned them about the instability of the foundations of Gwrtheyrn's building. They were unable to answer. Then the young child told them the answer. He said that under the floor of the foundations lay a pool, and in the pool were two vases. Between the vases there was a pavilion or tent, and in the tent were two serpents or dragons (**16**). One was white and the other red. They started to fight with each other. At first the white dragon was winning but weakened and was at length overcome by the red dragon. This amazed everyone but greater was their wonder when the little boy went on to interpret the meaning of this vision. He said that the red dragon represented Gwrtheyrn's followers and the white dragon was the emblem of the Saxons. They were fighting because they both wanted victory and the fact that the white dragon represented the Saxons showed that in time this race would be driven back across the sea to their own country; and the red dragon indicated that the triumphant Vortigern should now build his stronghold in another place. There seems to be quite a lot of confusion in this tale but the fundamental significance of it is clear.

Merlin appears in Geoffrey of Monmouth's *Historia Regum Britanniae* as prophet and magician, with some input from both local traditions and Nennius the chronicler. Geoffrey (twelfth-century and perhaps a Breton by birth) describes him as having been born to a nun who was a daughter of the king of Demetia, fathered by an incubus. His birth allegedly took place in the city of Carmarthen, the Welsh for which is Caerfyrddin, 'Myrddin's town', but this is thought to be an incorrect etymology. In Geoffrey's *Vita Merlini*, *Life of Merlin*, as well as in the Welsh texts, Merlin figures as a prophet who lived in North Britain in the sixth century. In medieval Wales it was popular to attribute many mantic poems to Merlin, none of which, however, were earlier than Geoffrey. It is believed that they pertain to a much earlier tradition of the 'Wild Man of the Woods', which was known throughout the British Isles. Merlin's mantic powers often threatened his sanity and drove him to behave like one suffering from

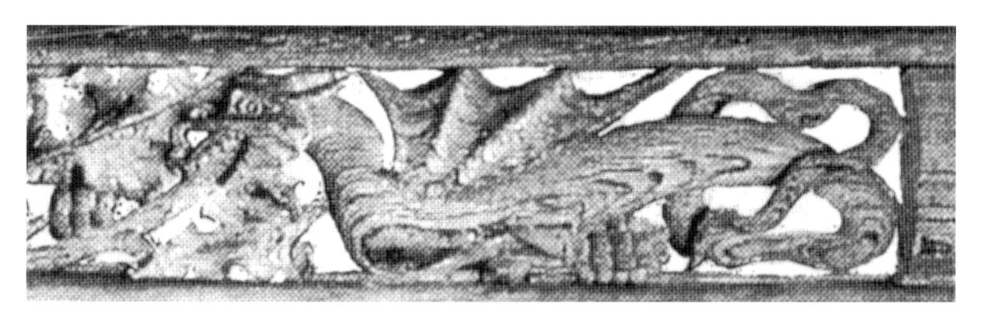

16 *Dragon eating foliage on roodscreen of about AD 1500 in the church of St Issui or Ishow, Partrishow, Powys. After C. Kightly* A Travellers Guide to Places of Worship, *London, 1986, p.93*

dementia. Early legend depicts him as living in the Caledonian Forest of Scotland in a wretched state of madness and despair, all of which had been brought about by his unnerving powers of 'seeing', that is, of seeing into the future, with its horrors and human suffering. This mental disturbance was allegedly exaggerated by the battle of Arfderydd (one of the 'Three Futile Battles' according to the Triad — *vide TYP* pp.208-10) during which Merlin, 'bitter and enraged', joined the 'wild men of the mountains' (*Arthur of the Welsh* p.119).

Merlin has attained to universal popularity on account of his colourful and often tragic career, his association with the legendary King Arthur and his knights, the creation of the elusive Round Table, and the excitement and tragedy of the prophecies which so sadly almost destroyed the prophet.

5 The Church and the oral tradition in Wales

Giraldus Cambrensis or Gerald of Wales was seemingly born in or around AD 1145-6. He was brought up on the coast of Pembrokeshire, South Wales, in the castle of Manorbier, which he vividly describes in the *Journey through Wales*. He was the son of a Norman knight, William de Barry. The name was adopted by his family after an island off the Glamorgan coast, Barry Island. He had a Welsh mother, Angharad, daughter of Nest and granddaughter of Rhys ap Tewdwr, Prince of South Wales. Angharad's father was a Norman knight named Gerald of Windsor, so Angharad was only half Welsh. Gerald himself was three-quarters Norman. David Fitzgerald, a brother of Angharad, became Bishop of St David's in 1148 and as a result of this influence Gerald was expected to enter the Church. This he did with great distinction. He had an astute mind and was not afraid to record virtually verbatim many interesting items of folklore and early tradition even when these were more apposite to paganism than to the narrow view of Christianity then pertaining. He travelled widely and in 1184 he was appointed by Henry II to be Court chaplain and spent some time in Ireland. His visit led to the creation of two famous books, namely *The Topography of Ireland* (*Topographia Hibernica*) and *The Conquest of Ireland* (*Ex Pugnatio Hibernica*).

He made many pilgrimages and lengthy journeys preaching the Christian message, visiting the cathedrals of Llandaff, St David's, Bangor and St Asaph until 1188. These peregrinations he describes in his third book, *Itinerarium Kambriae* (*The Journey through Wales*). Four times Gerald had refused a bishopric, twice in Ireland and twice in Wales. The reason for this was his ardent wish for one see alone, that of St David's. In 1199 King John succeeded to the throne at Westminster. He then sent for Gerald and seemingly informed him that he intended to create him bishop. In June 1199 Gerald went to St David's, where he was unanimously made bishop-elect. This, however, did not come to fruition and many years of travel and hazards were to ensue. His dream was never realised and he died at an advanced age in 1223.

Giraldus is of great interest for many aspects of medieval Welsh history and even includes in his works some fascinating details of certain superstitious folk beliefs and traces of archaic customs alongside his more austere preoccupations. For example, during his travels he was informed about historical events pertaining to particular localities to supernatural happenings or objects of a ghostly or miraculous nature and this plethora of events led him on many occasions to deviate from the subject. He shows a considerable interest in belief in poltergeists and evidence for their existence. He also notes several objects which were accredited with magical power; a staff, for example, which once allegedly belonged to St Curig was kept in the church of St Germanus in the district of Gwrtherynion — a commote of southern Powys. The staff was encased in gold and silver and the top cruciform in shape. It had proven miraculous powers, in particular its healing of certain tumours of the body. People suffering from such distressing ailments were believed to be healed if they approached the holy staff with total faith in its healing properties and made an offering of a small sum of money. All 'miracle' healing requires complete faith in order to succeed. It happened in Giraldus' time that a man, suffering from a tumour, offered the crozier a halfpenny. This resulted in the healing of only one half of his lesion. Not long afterwards, he hastened to offer the staff the second halfpenny, and was at once completely healed.

A miraculous hand-bell (known as Bangu) was housed in Glascwm Church in Elfael, Radnorshire. It too was allegedly possessed of miraculous powers. It was said to have belonged to St David and, according to tradition, had been brought to the church by supernatural oxen as a gift from the saint (Dewi Sant). A local tradition has it that a certain woman took it to Rhayader, believing that her husband, who was imprisoned in the castle, would be freed when she rang it, but the bell was seized by guards and she was refused entry. That night a great fire destroyed the whole town apart from the wall on which the bell had been hung.

On the night when King Henry I died a strange occurrence happened in the Elfael district, which lies to the north of Hay-on-Wye. There were two large pools nearby, one man-made, the other occurring naturally. As is frequently recorded before the death of some royal or eminent person, a marvellous event took place. The two pools suddenly rose and burst their banks. The artificial pool rushed down the valleys and of course was soon empty of water. Strangely, the natural pool recreated itself some two miles away, complete with its fish and other aquatic life.

Giraldus Cambrensis, still on the theme of the supernatural, records that in his own day in parts of Pembroke, 'unclean spirits' were believed to have been in communication with human beings. These he describes as being invisible, but their presence could clearly be felt. The poltergeists would for example indulge in annoying acts such as throwing various items of rubbish throughout the house with seemingly an intention of causing only nuisance.

They would rip up and damage people's clothes, and nothing could keep them away from these, even when the doors were thoroughly barred against them. In other cases, even stranger occurrences happened, with the spirits habitually arguing with the inhabitants. When the people objected the spirit would silence them by publicly reciting every nasty little deed they had committed from the time of their birth. These were things they did not like to be made public!

> St David's cathedral was founded in honour of St Andrew the Apostle. The place where it stands is called the valley of the roses (*Vallis Rosina*). A better name for it would be the valley of marble, for it is in no sense rosy or remarkable for roses, whereas there are plenty of rocks all over the place. The churchyard is bounded on the north side by the River Alun, a muddy and unproductive stream. It runs under the Llech Lafar Stone (*lapidae Lechlavar*) which means the talking stone, a slab of marble polished by the feet of those innumerable people who have walked across it. I have written about the size, texture and name of this stone in my *Vaticinal History* (i.e. the conquest of Ireland). What follows is my description of how Henry II, King of the English, crossed over this stone on his return from Ireland, as he went into the cathedral of St Andrew and St David to pray . . . Dressed as a pilgrim, on foot and leaning on a staff, he went into St David's Cathedral to pray . . . As a procession advanced, the clergy, walking one by one and with proper ceremony, a Welsh woman threw herself at the king's feet and made a complaint about the Bishop of St David's. Nothing could be done there and then . . . so she gestured violently with her hands and, with everyone listening, had the impudence to shout in a loud voice; 'Revenge us today, Llech Lafar! Revenge the whole Welsh people on this man!' She was held back and then driven away by those who understood the Welsh language. As she went she shouted even more loudly and violently. She repeated the well-known fiction and prophecy of Merlin, so often heard, that a king of England who had just conquered Ireland, would be wounded in that country by a man with a red hand, and then on his return to St David's would die as he walked over Llech Lafar. This was the name of the stone which served as a bridge over the River Alun, a stream which marks the boundary of the cemetery on the north side of the cathedral . . . It was ten feet long, six feet wide and one foot deep . . . There is an age-old legend about this stone that once, when the corpse was being carried across it, it burst into speech and in the effort split down

> the middle, the crack still being visible today. Because of this heathen superstition, attributed to the stone in bygone days, they have given up carrying corpses across it. It so happened that the King knew all about the prophecy. When he reached the stone he stopped and eyed it closely. Then, without further hesitation, he walked boldly over it. As soon as he was across he turned round, glared at the stone, and with no small indignation, made this trenchant remark about the soothsayer: 'Merlin is a liar. Who will trust him now?' A wit, who was there among the crowd, heard the king's remark and pretended to take umbrage at the insult offered to the prophet. 'You are not the king who is to conquer Ireland', he said. 'Merlin was not talking about you at all.'
> (Giraldus Cambrensis, *The Description of Wales* trans. Lewis Thorpe)

This passage is not only of particular interest because of the reference to the prophecy of Merlin, but because of that to the legend of the *llech lafar* or talking stone. We meet with such a tradition again in *The Fifteen Signs Before Doomsday* by William W. Heist. The ninth sign before the doom is invariably conceived as the moment when all the stones begin to speak. In some versions not only are the stones said to speak but each stone splits up into three parts and all of these begin to fight. As far as I am aware, however, in all the varied references to the Doom, it is on the ninth day that this disturbing event takes place. (cf. MacKendrick, P., 1962)

Awenyddion 'Welsh soothsayers'

Giraldus has some quite interesting and potentially important comments to make on this group of inspired Welsh people. They bear, from his descriptions, a considerable similarity to those Scottish Highlanders believed to possess a form of foreknowledge known as *fiosaiche*. Giraldus describes the way in which the Welsh soothsayers are 'taken over' by this trance-like state, in which present reality disappears to be replaced by visions, often expressed in speech having more or less coherency. He states that the *awenyddion* 'behave as if they are possessed by devils'. He also states that you will find them nowhere else, which as we have seen is not quite the case, although the two are not absolutely identical. He describes them in the following terms:

> When you consult them about some problem, they immediately go into a trance and lose control of their senses as if they are

> possessed. They do not answer the question put to them in any logical way. Words stream from their mouths, incoherently and apparently meaningless and without any sense at all, but all the same well-expressed: and if you listen carefully to what they say you will receive the solution to your problem. When it is all over, they will recover from their trance as if they were ordinary people waking from a heavy sleep, but you have to give them a good shake before they regain control of themselves . . . when they do return to their senses they can remember nothing of what they said . . . It is possible that they are speaking through demons which possess them, spirits which are ignorant and yet in some way inspired.

Here Giraldus skilfully conveys to the reader interesting glimpses of the way in which the *awenyddion* were 'taken over' by some powerful yet invisible force which enabled them to make convincing prophetic utterances. Every Celtic community had its 'seer' usually possessing the powers of prophecy or of 'second sight', such as was highly developed amongst the Scottish Highlanders.

Giraldus refers to a pseudo-historical and a fictional King Arthur. Giraldus was one of the first, if not the first, to imagine that there were two Merlins, one the magician and soothsayer, and a second and older Merlin whose prophecies he himself discovered when he was in Nefyn with Archbishop Baldwin. He drew attention to the fact that Gildas, in his *De Excidio Britanniae* (book II, 2, 628) never mentioned Arthur. Arthur's tomb (Glastonbury Abbey) seems irrelevant for this book, but if required see Appendix 3 p.281.

Giraldus has much to say about the important qualities of Anglesey, in North Wales. For example:

> When crops have failed in all other regions, this island, from the richness of its soil and its abundant produce, has been able to supply all Wales. You will find much on Anglesey which is worthy of your attention. I have thought it a good idea to choose a few of these features and to insert a description of them here. There is, for example, a stone almost in the shape of a human thigh-bone which has this extraordinary property, so often proved true by the local inhabitants, that however far away it is carried, it returns of its own accord the following night. [NB this belongs to a widespread and varied tradition of the magical return of venerated objects that had been stolen, for example the church bells at Killin.] 'Huw, Earl of Shrewsbury

17 *'Fair gull on the warm tide-flow.' Dafydd ap Gwilym*

> who, in the reign of King Henry I forcibly occupied the whole island . . . heard of the properties of this stone. To test it, he had it attached by iron chains to a much larger stone and then thrown far out to sea. Early the next morning, to everyone's astonishment, they found it back again in its usual place, to which it always returned. The Earl issued a public edict that no-one from this time onwards should remove it from its place. But in another attempt to test the stone, a countryman had it tied to his own thigh. His leg became gangrenous, but the stone returned to its place.

Thomas Pennant was born in 1726 in Flintshire and died in 1798. He received a varied education, studying at Wrexham, then in London and Oxford. He was fascinated by natural history and geology, and with these interests in mind, made detailed tours in, amongst other places, the Celtic countries of Wales, Ireland and Scotland. His comments are always of interest; his folklore anecdotes are invaluable.

Pennant, in his account of his journey to Snowdon (Vol. II, 1781) has the following to say about the westerly point of the Lleyn Peninsula:

18 *View of Bardsey Island. T. Pennant, 1780, pl.13*

> In a small time I reached Aberdaron, a poor village at the very end of Caernarvonshire, seated on a sandy bay, beneath some high and sandy cliffs. The mouth of the bay is guarded by two little islands, called Ynys Gwylan (fawr and bâch) ('Seagull Island') (**17**), as security to the small craft of the inhabitants, who were all fishermen. It takes its name from the small rivulet, the Daron, which empties itself here.

One Ynys Gwylan was used as a stopping point by Christians taking the boat across to Bardsey, Ynys Enlli (**18**), which was extremely popular with pilgrims and a place where many holy men desired to receive burial. That this frequently happened is suggested by the tradition that more than 20,000 saints are buried there. The island is some two miles in circumference (**19**) and a small number of people have always resided there. At the present time the remaining dwellings are rented out to people who wish to seek peace there in a place where they can spend time in reflection. A boat calls weekly, bringing provisions.

The Lleyn Peninsula off the end of which Bardsey is located probably takes its name from the Laigin, the men of Leinster in Ireland who are reputed to have settled there somewhere in the fifth or sixth centuries AD. One has only to drive to the beginning of the peninsula to note that the

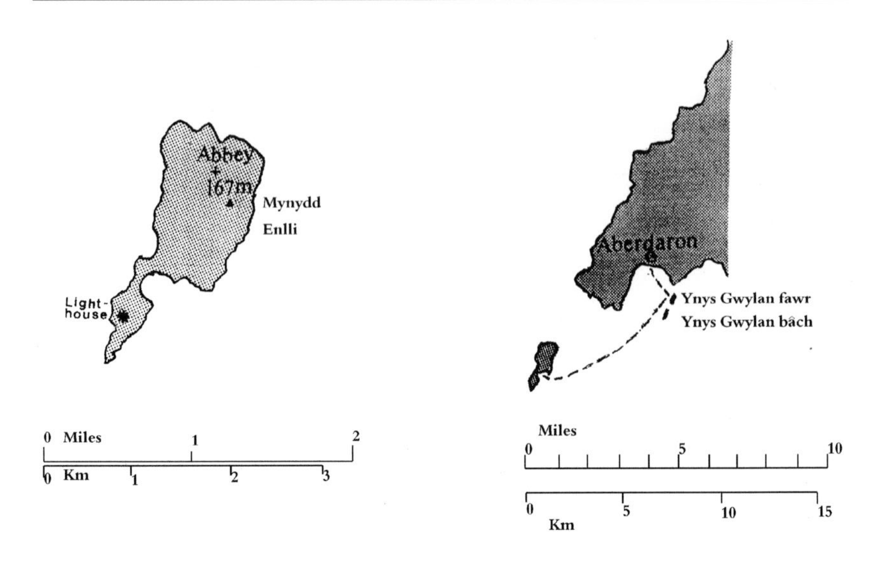

19 Ynys Enlli, *Bardsey Island, Gwynedd, and approach from Aberdaron*

fields are a patchwork of small walled enclosures reminiscent of the Irish field systems. This is but one example of the powerful impact of the Irish on the landscape of Wales. There are numerous other examples of an Irish presence here. Even in the hilly countryside in the midst of which I live there are remains of small stone dwellings known in Welsh as *cytiau'r Gwyddelod*, 'Irish huts'.

6 Severed heads, saints, sacred waters and stones

Celtic heads; heads in waters

There was a close association throughout the Celtic countries between severed heads and sacred waters such as wells, lakes, pools and fords. The Welsh tradition would appear to be less rich in this respect that that of Scotland or Ireland but this may not be the case. Only intensive research over a wide area will serve to verify this. That is not to say that there are no traces of such a cult in Wales and the literary and folklore traditions do lend some support to this aspect of the cult in Wales. On several occasions I have driven to places in Wales at the request of people who have discovered stone heads or heads in other materials on or near their own properties. One of these was at Llanbrynmair, Powys (**20**). The houses are built close to the powerful River Twymyn. Some years ago one of the residents of the pretty houses close to the water was making a rockery in his garden and he wanted a river stone of a certain size to put in it. He knew where he would find one and he duly lifted the sizeable boulder from the water and took it back to his garden. There it lay until he was ready to put it in place. When he turned it over he received a considerable shock. The reverse side of the stone, which was somewhat head-shaped, was already carved with a human face. He got such a fright that he almost dropped the stone. The owner of the land, who had read some of my books in which I had discussed the severed head and its implications, telephoned me and asked me to come and see this extraordinary find. This I did as soon as I was able and was taken to view the stone. It was indeed an impressive carving, possibly dating to the early decades of the first century AD.

Its presence in the water would not by any means be unparalleled. Severed heads or representations of such seem always to have had a close association with water. It would seem that the head was believed to increase the powers of the water and that the water had a similar effect upon the head. I believe that the head is now in the possession of the National Museum of Wales in Cardiff. It is not necessary for me to wander far afield in search of heads. Rhydypennau (some two miles from where I live) means 'the Ford of the Heads'. The name itself is evocative considering this Celtic motif of severed

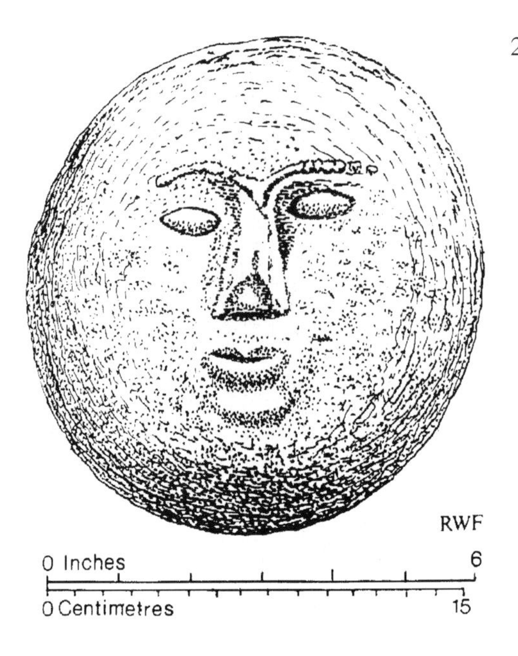

20 *Llanbrynmair, Montgomeryshire. Features in low relief on a waterworn pebble found in the River Twymyn at Bont, Llanbrynmair, in 1971*

heads and sacred waters, but the story does not end here. Some years ago, when work was being carried out on the Nant Ceiro (which runs through our grounds), three heads were allegedly found in the old ford. I have not been able as yet to ascertain whether these were stone heads or actual human skulls. However, the association of severed heads with fords is widely known in the Celtic world.

A most important Celtic head, fashioned from coarse-grained sandstone, and having a remarkably disturbing aspect, was apparently found in a, to date, unconfirmed site near Llandysul, Ceredigion. The head was dug up in farmland close to Llandysul (**21**) before the Second World War and was later auctioned in London. Although the exact provenance is not known, an important point to bear in mind is the fact that the coarse-grained sandstone from which it is carved is common in the Llandysul/Pencader area. Moreover the weathering of the stone would be consistent with a lengthy period of burial. It is basically a rectangular block, somewhat rounded with a well-defined chin, full-lipped mouth, slightly drooping. The eyes, which have a sunken appearance, are encircled by heavily-defined, 'fleshy' ridges. Many Celtic heads are depicted as having one eye either lacking altogether or smaller than the other and having baleful powers of evil, and this would appear to be the case here. The most impressive textual description of such a phenomenon occurs in the early Irish story of the god, Balor, *Beumshuileach*, Balor of the evil eye, grandfather of the pan-Celtic god Lugh. What is to be the ultimate fate of this splendid artefact which sadly has left Wales but is in

21 Llandysul, Ceredigion. Head of coarse-grained sandstone

safe keeping elsewhere, we do not know. It would, however, be appropriate if, one day, it were to return to its place of apparent origin.

There is a very graphic description of heads taken in battle during the reign of James II when there was great unrest in the country, especially in Flintshire. Near here, at Balderton Bridge, the thorough defeat of the Welsh by the Earl of Chester was followed by acts of great cruelty. The Earl publicised his triumph by creating a rampart of the severed heads of the enemy. This distasteful sequel to the battle and brutal treatment of the defeated is fully in keeping with the ethos of the time. The severed heads so treated are typical of Celtic practice down the ages when victory was proclaimed by the display and even veneration of the severed heads of those who fell in battle (*vide* Ross, Druids).

Heads on Anglesey (*Ynys Môn*); the Hendy head

Anglesey is a significant island in terms of Celtic religion and mythology, traces of both of which are still very much in evidence. Situated as it is a short distance from the north-west coast of Wales and joined to the mainland now by an efficient road bridge, Anglesey nevertheless has managed to preserve to a surprising extent some very ancient traditions and artefacts — especially carved stone heads — some of which may well go back to an early period in legend and perhaps also in material origin.

22 Head of red sandstone from Hendy, Môn

One of the most remarkable stone heads is not only important as a cult object, but, unusually, has a great deal of archaic and remarkably interesting tradition attached to it, which until very recently was kept a close secret. When I first saw the head I was visiting Anglesey for other reasons — Llyn Cerrig Bach, the Druids, and holy wells. I had been informed that there was a very interesting head at Hendy and, on being given directions from a local man, thought it as well to try to locate it whilst I was there. The directions were good, and I soon found myself looking at this impressive stone head set upon a stone wall (**22**). The encounter gave me quite a shock. I had been prepared for a substantial object but not for the tremendous power which seemed to emanate from it, which I did not anticipate. The mouth, slightly upturned at the corners, is not a smiling mouth; it has a sinister quality which is emphasised by the extraordinary lentoid eyes with their protruding irises and well-defined pupils, cut deep under the severe brows which serve to increase the strong impact of the stone on the viewer. The nose is long and narrow, broadening towards the nostrils, the remains of which are just visible; some areas of the red sandstone, which seemingly comes from the region of Lligwy, are better preserved than others and there is quite a lot of flaking of the stone. There is one well-preserved ear which resembles a crescent in shape. The second ear is less well-formed and the stone appears to have been damaged at some time in the past. The lipped and enigmatic mouth with its non-smile bears a striking feature which is seen on some of the earliest Celtic stone heads in Europe, and is known as a 'cigarette hole'.

The most well-known is that found at Mšecké- Ž ehrovice, near Prague (**23**). Made of ragstone and exhibiting, in a more elaborate form, features which bear a sophisticated similarity to those of the Hendy example, each head has a detail which seems to occur over a wide area of Europe and to have some definite religious or cultic significance. This is the deep hole drilled into the middle of the upper lip in the case of the Bohemian head, and into the corner of the mouth in the case of the Hendy head. This lends an even more sinister quality to the whole and in general such features are thought to have been fashioned in order that the voice of the deity might be heard through them. Be that as it may, and whatever interpretation we may accept, there is no doubt that they did have a purpose. We are fortunate to actually know what that purpose is in the case of the Hendy head, which even today is used in an ancient cult ritual in Anglesey. The meetings which are held in connection with what we can only call the veneration of this head are quite complex, and full details, in so far as we have access to them, can be found in chapter 11.

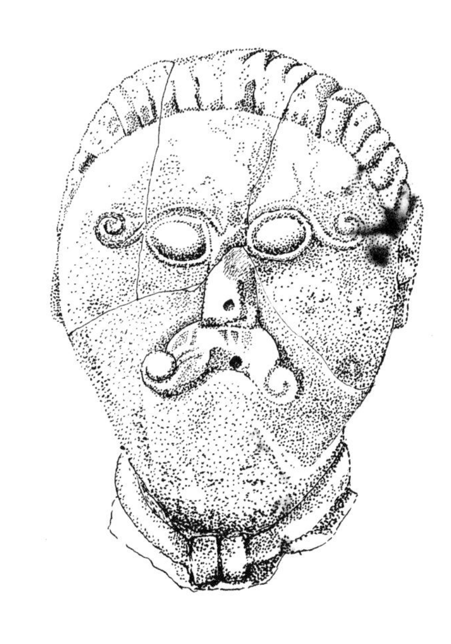

23 Stone head, Mšecké - Žehrovice, Bohemia

The rite which explains the presence of the deep hole ('cigarette hole') in the corner of the head's mouth occurred in the ceremony after the stone, which is some 2ft in height, had been placed on a table and covered with a white cloth. The cloth was removed from the head and one of the 'worshippers' placed cheese and bayleaves on the flat summit of the head. Next an object like a tube, called the *stwffwl cist uffern* ('staple for hell's chest') was placed in the hole. This enabled the head to 'breathe its blessings' upon the group. Each person in succession put the tube in the head's mouth. I believe that the tube concealed a piece of paper on which some words were written and this was believed to be of very ancient origin.

The Brynsiencin head

One May day on a morning of sublime beauty I went to a house in this village in order to try to locate another stone head which I had been informed was kept in a garden there. I managed to locate the property and found the owners most hospitable and anxious to help me in my quest. I was taken out to the back yard of the house and there in a corner at the end of the yard I saw a most striking sight; a large stone head with well-depicted features, known to the family as *yr Hen Ŵr* ('the Old Man'; **24**). The tradition of scrubbing and cleaning the moss from such heads, but not, in this case, painting them, had already been carried out and this fine carving looked impressive and impassive, despite having a slightly sinister aspect.

24 A stone at Brynsiencyn, Môn, with a face carved on either side in the janiform manner. Attention was drawn to the stone by the owner, Mrs M. Brownson, in 1971

The family was very hospitable and welcoming and we had a long talk over tea and cake. I was told an interesting story about this head. Seemingly a member of the family had enquired why the front of this substantial stone was so carefully cleaned and 'made smart' for May Day, while the back of the stone received no such attention. The owners had therefore decided to give it the same treatment and, with help from others, the large carved stone was slowly turned round and the reverse side cleaned. Great was the astonishment of the owners when they found a second, smaller face carved on the reverse side; the stone was in fact janiform. It had been present in that position for many years without any one suspecting or questioning the presence of a second head. Anglesey is certainly not lacking in stone sculptures of this kind and there are others which are probably likewise of an early date, although dating by style alone can be problematic.

Other Anglesey heads

Although somewhat later in date, the tradition of using carved stone heads of a markedly pagan aspect but built into Christian structures seems to have survived until at least the fourteenth century. We cannot treat this subject with the fullness it deserves here but the following examples will give an indication of the tradition.

25 Llanddyfnan church, Môn. Head over north doorway

One of the most interesting of these is set into the wall above the door of Llanddyfnan Church (**25**). It is a head having a flat top which may have been due to the necessity of lowering its height to fit into its position above the doorway. The double-rimmed lentoid eyes, flattish nose, severe straight-lipped mouth and full, rounded chin combined with the sturdy neck suggest a commanding and somewhat sinister power. The arms, raised in an orans attitude, suffer from a considerable degree of weathering: it is not impossible that this head is much older than the church structure, and was possibly dug up on the site when the building was being constructed and incorporated into it as so often happened. Perhaps a latent belief in the all-powerful Celtic head cult allowed pagan carvings to use their evil-averting qualities for the good of the church itself.

There are several other fine heads of this genre. In the case of abandoned, ruined churches I came across some carved boulders or building blocks which had obviously been placed in the wall with the face looking into the church, perhaps in the belief that this would strengthen their evil-averting powers. Other splendid heads, the date of which is difficult to ascertain, are built into churches such as the pair at Llanidan (see **4**), which appear to have cleft beards, long narrow noses and lips which are half-opened as if in speech. Legends of talking heads are by no means unknown in the Celtic tradition. A head at Llanbedrgoch (**26**) is set on the right of the doorway and likewise has a commanding presence. The eyebrows are deeply cut away and the protruding eyes have extremely well-defined pupils in the form of two large hollows. The nose is long and thin. The head gives the impression of being

26a Llanbedrgoch church, Môn. Head embedded in plaster to the right of the doorway

pointed but this may well be due to the fact that the cement with which it was presumably set into the church wall has had the effect of conveying the illusion of an unnaturally high forehead with markings above which might indicate hair. Be this as it may, and whatever the dates of these Anglesey church heads, they do convey a strong impression of the superstitious regard in which the head was held in Anglesey.

Going back to a pagan context, it is worth mentioning the Blessed Head, the severed head of Bendigeidfran, 'Bran the Blessed' (See I. Williams 1930, pp.44ff), which was first taken by his distraught sister, Branwen, and the remaining Welshmen who had survived the terrible battle, to Anglesey, where they landed at Aberalaw. The knowledge that two fine countries, Wales and Ireland, had been virtually destroyed because of her so distressed Branwen that her heart broke in her breast and she died. She was, according to the tradition, buried on the banks of the River Alaw. Some years ago an excavation was carried out at the site which tradition associated with Branwen's interment. There was disappointment when a Bronze Age coffin was recovered and it was rejected as having been the burial place of Bran's sister. However, if these legends have drawn upon immensely archaic traditions there would seem to be no reason for rejecting this apparent verification of the medieval Welsh text. We follow the progress of the Blessed Head in another context and turn again to remaining sites on Anglesey which may be of interest to our investigation.

26b Llanbedrgoch church, Môn. Head embedded in plaster to the left of the doorway

A site which was of great importance for the free Celtic world is located at Llyn Cerrig Bach (the Lake of the Little Stones, near Holyhead, Anglesey). Here the free (i.e. before being conquered by the Romans) Celtic tribes, fleeing from the advancing Roman troops, made one last desperate attempt to gain the favourable intervention of the gods on their behalf. Many objects which can only be regarded as offerings and coming from different parts of Britain and Ireland were recovered here at the time of the building of the airfield for the Second World War. Those articles which were of Irish origin are of special interest and I have suggested elsewhere (*Druids*) that this may have been a chief pagan sanctuary in Britain. Moving eastwards to Penmon which today is close to where the modern bridge links the mainland to Anglesey we come to a silvan site where the ruins of a priory still stand. The place is densely wooded and the ruins of the sixth-century priory are still to be found there. The atmosphere is serene and there is a feeling of holiness. Strangely, on the wall of part of the priory still standing is carved a *sheelagh-na-gig* (a female fertility symbol), and such images, male and female, are by no means unusual in early church architecture. Their purpose was probably to scare away evil spirits. The priory fishpond and well are still in existence.

Many other Celtic heads occur in Wales; see, for example **27**, **28**, **29**, **30**, **31**.

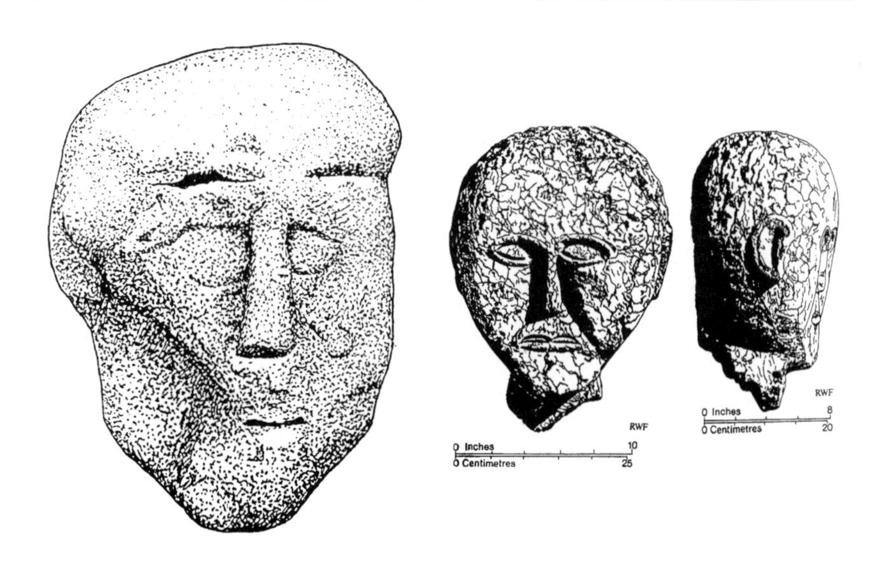

27 *Stone head from CANOVIVM, Caerhun, Gwynedd. After A. Ross 1967, fig.56*

28 *Ruthin, Denbighshire. This head was found in 1973 near a waterfall a little over 1km ESE of Ruthin castle; Landranger 116, SJ 112574. It is in the Merseyside County Museum, William Brown Street, Liverpool*

29 *Two stone heads, one janiform, from Bron y Garth, a mile south of Chirk castle but half a mile east of Offa's Dyke and thus in Shropshire rather than Clwyd*

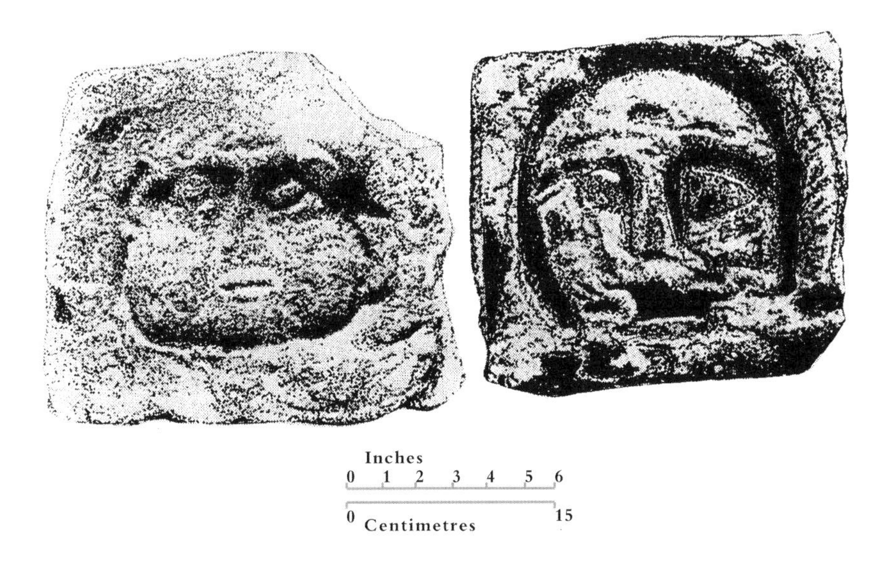

30 Faces carved in relief on stones. (left) Holt, Clwyd, (right) Maridvnvm, Carmarthen. After A. Ross 1967, pl.29

31 Stone head from Venta Silvrvm, Caerwent, Gwent. After A. Ross 1967, pl.31a

The well cult

The association of severed human heads or skulls with wells, certain of which have distinctive properties of their own such as healing powers, is very ancient, common to the early Celtic world in general, and with a variety of associations. Heads fashioned of stone, metal or other substances would often act as a substitute for the human or animal skull; the powers of the severed head, when united with sacred water from the well, were greatly increased and enhanced. There are many tales throughout the Celtic world of this fundamental belief in the power of the severed head to continue living, moving, and sometimes singing, talking, cursing or perhaps blessing. Heads were frequently associated with holy wells patronised by some saint or another and they also were able to prophesy future events or to recall the past. Indeed their powers would seem to have been limitless. In a book such as this, space must inevitably dictate the nature of content, and I cannot give as many examples of such wells as I would wish. I have selected, however, a few that I consider to be explanatory and of prime importance. Wells were often created at the moment of the martyrdom of some important saint. Saints after this grim fate could be portrayed as carrying their severed heads, which were ultimately lodged in the well for which they had been responsible.

Saints and wells (32)

One of the most fascinating aspects of pagan and Christian religion is the rôle played by wells and springs. There are many stories of some god or goddess, monstrous beast or malevolent serpent having power over wells, sometimes living in them and acting as guardian for the wellbeing of those who invoked them. According to belief, every sacred well and spring must be treated with appropriate respect — and even those with no traditions attached must be accorded due honour or they would be capable of drying up or moving to another site. A murdered virgin is sometimes said to have been restored to life and to have lived for many years after her murder at or near her sacred well or chapel.

At one healing well, stones were present which were stained with red patches and these were explained as being stains from the blood of a Catholic priest who was decapitated there in Queen Elizabeth's time. Stones carrying the bloodstains of martyred saints were also sometimes recovered, for example at St Winifred's well (*vide* infra p.81) and St Michael's well in Monmouthshire. White quartz stones or pebbles had their own sanctity and when thrown into a well as offerings at times of drought it was widely believed that there would be water in plenty. In the Scottish Highlands such

32 Higgon's Well, Hwlffordd (Haverfordwest), Pembrokeshire. After S. Rees 1992, p.197

stones, when cast into wells by people with supernatural powers, could cause the well to flood and overflow, or raise a storm at sea, according to the correct invocation. One of the most interesting wells is that on Caldey Island (Ynys Bŷr), near Tenby, Pembrokeshire, where there has been a monastery since the sixth century. It was first named after St Illtud, but it later became known as Ynys Bŷr. There is a tale telling how Pyr, or Pyro, the abbot, was supposed to have died by falling into a well while under the influence of strong drink. St Samson succeeded him and found he had taken on an almost impossible task. Pyr had been a very dissolute abbot and the young monks under his tutelage were virtually uncontrollable. As a result Samson was so shocked that he gave up the abbacy shortly afterwards.

I visited Caldey a few days ago (June 2001) and my friend, Brother Gildas, took me to the spot where Pyro's well was situated, close to a lake full of leaping carp and bright with flowers. The past feels very much in the present here on this timeless island with its long history of Christian sanctity.

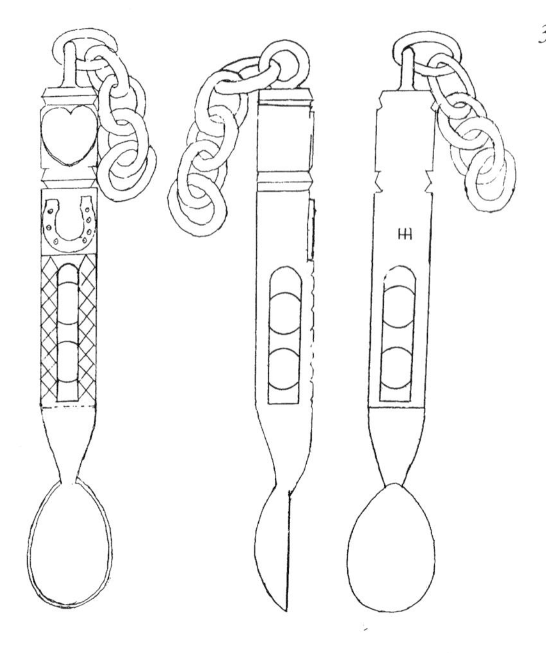

33 A wooden love spoon made in the traditional way by Huw Hughes of Felin Gyffin. The art of under-cutting is demonstrated by the five links from which the spoon may be suspended, and the chamber in the body of the spoon in which two spheres roll freely — all made by cutting them free from the surrounding wood

St Dwynwen's well

St Dwynwen, who lived in the fifth century, was the daughter of Brychan who was both saint and king. She was therefore of high birth. She is looked upon in Wales as the patron saint of lovers (**33**) and her feast day occurs on 25 January. She is closely connected with Môn (Anglesey), and there are places and wells which still bear her name. A spring called Ffynnon Dwynwen is situated close to the church of Llanddwyn. People who have been crossed in love or wish to arouse an amorous response in the heart of the one they love resort to this well and make a wish there in the belief that their desire will be fulfilled. Some years ago when I was staying with a friend near Bethesda I went to Anglesey on a warm summer's day with the purpose, amongst other things, of visiting St Dwynwen's Well. It was a scene of incredible beauty; the great mountains reaching down towards the sea; and the smell of summer flowers filled the air as we walked upon the lush green grass towards the well. The whole island had a timeless quality and one could sense the sanctity of the site and almost feel the passionate pleadings of those who longed to have their love returned. The great medieval poet, Dafydd ap Gwilym, whose birthplace and much of whose life occurred very close to where I live, with only a hill separating us from his family home, made a pilgrimage to this sweet spring and a wish that his — current — beloved would respond to his ardour.

St Winifred's well

St Winifred was also known as Gwenffrewi, Gwenfrewy and Winefred (seventh century). Her Life (*Buchedd*) is not by any means truly historical but has attracted to itself numerous fragments or elements of folklore. It is often difficult to separate the two. She was of high birth; her father (Tyfid) belonged to Englefield (Tegeingl), in Flintshire, and her mother Gwenlo was the daughter of Insi, King of Powys. St Beuno, who is connected with Clynnog Fawr, Caernarfonshire, and whose cult seems to have been in North Wales as well (e.g. in Anglesey), was seemingly her uncle. She is supposed to have been raped and killed by one Caradog, a prince. She had been decapitated but her uncle, Beuno, immediately replaced her head on her body and she was restored to life. There were seemingly few physical traces of her violent 'death', save for a thin red line round her neck where the head had been struck off.

Her well is situated in beautiful wooded country below the town of Treffynon, known today as Holywell. The spring rushes out of a rock and is channelled into a built well with many fine architectural features. At some stage Winifred went on a pilgrimage to Rome and there is a tradition that she performed numerous miracles during her lifetime. She was so popular that she is commemorated in the works of several Welsh poets and Holywell after her death became a place renowned for pilgrimages, especially frequented by Roman Catholics. The popularity of Holywell has continued right down to the present time. It is known as one of the Seven Wonders of Wales.

St Tecla's Well

The village of Llandegla, Clwyd is renowned for the presence of a potent well, known as St Tecla's Well and widely famed for its powers of healing epilepsy. We do not know a great deal about St Tecla but she is described by Pennant (Vol. I, 1784, p.405) as being both virgin and martyr. She was converted to Christianity by St Paul and thereafter was put to death by Nero. Whether this is the same saint or not is in question. However that may be, she certainly achieved a wide popularity on account of the powers of her well in curing the widespread disease of epilepsy, known in Gaelic as *Tinneas tuiteam*, 'the falling disease', which was also very common in the Scottish Highlands. The Welsh terms for epilepsy are *haint digwydd* or *gewynglwyf*. Situated in beautiful wooded countryside is the church of St Tecla; about 200 yards from this is the holy well, the water of which rises from a place called Gwern Degla. The sacred water is under the protection of the saint, and people still believe in its powers to heal the distressing ailment.

Visiting the well after a service in the nearby church a few years ago, I was much impressed by the sense of peace and holiness which seemed still to prevail. In the past a patient seeking the cure must immerse his limbs in the water and wash them, then, in Pennant's time, make an offering into it of four pence, next walking round it three times while repeating the Lord's Prayer the same number of times. As is common for wells with the power to cure epilepsy in Scotland and Wales, the healing process begins only after sunset and must be completed before dawn. Pennant comments that this is in order to inspire the votaries with greater awe. I would not put quite the same interpretation on this as it is obviously a quieter time in which to perform rites which were not revealed to anyone other than the supplicant. The darkness would also add a sense of awe to the holy proceedings. During such healings the names of the Trinity were invariably invoked.

Offerings were still made well into the twentieth century and here they consisted of the sacrifice, by some means or another, of a cock; sometimes it was specified that the poor bird must be black. If the patient was male this bird would be appropriate, but if female then a hen would suffer the ultimate fate. The rite was carried out as follows: the bird was carried in a basket round the well (usually this circumambulation took place three times). Then it was carried into the churchyard and taken three times round the church. In Pennant's record (p.406, *op. cit.*) a somewhat strange performance then followed. The sick person would go into the church and get under the communion table. He would then lie down with the bible under his head. Next he would be covered with the altar carpet or cloth, and remain there until daybreak. At that time he would leave the church, presumably cured, first making an offering of six pence, and the poor cock was abandoned inside the church. Should the creature die, the cure was supposed to have been successful and the disease would be transferred to the devoted (i.e. offered, given up) victim. We are not told what the ultimate fate of the bird was, but it is not difficult to guess. Today the well is no longer used for this purpose.

Six stone heads were found in the vicinity of the well (**34**), and with our knowledge of the association of heads, stone or bone and healing waters one may hazard a guess that originally these played some part in the well cult. Be that as it may, they belonged to a local family at the time I visited Llandegla and were kept in front of the old stone house. The daughter of the house, a pleasant and helpful woman, told me that they were once used to secure the ropes and sheeting that served to cover the haystacks. It was shortly after May Day that I visited the house and the stones had just been painted black, which gave me quite a shock. On asking why this had been done I was told that because it was such an important time of year, when everything was being painted and cleaned for the approaching summer, it seemed proper to give the heads a coat of paint too, to 'smarten them up'. They used to stand in the porch of Rhos Ddigra, the old farmhouse. They have ears, but the backs of the heads are not worked. They are about 11in high.

34a Six stone heads from Llandegla, Clwyd

34b Compare these stone heads from the Gaulish Temple de la Forêt d'Halatte, Oise, France

Sometimes water was drunk out of human skulls. This custom may have arisen because of the belief that to drink out of a human skull, especially water from a sacred spring, would transfer its powers to the one who drank. The presence of the skull in such venerated water would increase the power, whatever it might be — fertility, healing, apotropaic qualities and the ability to ward off disease. The Celtic countries in general are well served by such venerated waters. Named wells occur widely throughout the Celtic world and have various beliefs and powers accredited to them. In Gaelic several wells are known as *tobar a'chinn*, 'the well of the head' or even with larger expanses of water the loch or lake of the head or heads. This is all in accordance with ancient Celtic belief that the severed head continued to live independently of the body. Wells of beheaded virgins occur in the lives of the saints. The basic story is as follows: the virgin flees from her would-be seducer; he captures her and decapitates her; a well springs up where the head or its blood fell. Sometimes the saint manages to restore the girl to life and she is able to live for many years afterwards. St Lludd was decapitated on Slwch Hill, Brecknockshire and 'her head, on rolling down the hill, caused a clear spring of water to issue out of the rock where it came to rest'. There was one well, Ffynnon Llandyfaen, in Carmarthenshire, where water was drunk out of a human skull, but by 1815 the reputation of the skull was almost lost. However the custom continued at a Pembrokeshire well and persisted until recent times.

St Teilo's Well, Ffynnon Deilo, which I heard called *Ffynnon yr Ychen* ('The Well of the Oxen') — this being its more common name locally — was famous for its waters which used to be drunk from St Teilo's skull (**35**) (*penglog Teilo*). A strong spring rises within a short distance of the ruined church of Llandilo-Isaf, near Maenchlochog, Pembrokeshire. It has a wide reputation as a healing well, and people come from long distances, just as they did to the epilepsy well at Torridon, West Highlands. The skull had to be dipped in the well, filled with water, and passed to the hereditary guardian. St Teilo died in AD 566. When dying, Teilo told his servant to take his skull from Llandeilo, Carmarthenshire, to Llandilo-Isaf, saying that by doing this he would be glorifying God and mankind would benefit. Jones also contributes the following information — a youth from Glamorgan who was ill with tuberculosis (about 1840) drank straight from the well in his eagerness to be healed, and went away without being cured. His father then took him back to the well and when he observed the correct ritual, and drank the water from the skull, the boy was completely restored to health. When I visited the well some years ago, the skull was kept in the farmhouse and still used for healing purposes.

The hereditary guardians, the Melchiors, came to Llandilo-Isaf through marriage in the second half of the seventeenth century. Trefor Owen states of the skull 'I regret to have to say that this relic has now disappeared'. It was actually taken to America, perhaps by someone claiming to be an ancestor, but it has now returned to Wales. Another spring, *ffynnon Fwy* ('the Well of Life'), Caernarfon, was subjected to abuse from a man who threw dead animals into it, resulting in the 'spirit' of the well taking offence. The water thereafter flowed up only in alternate years. They were fortunate it did not disappear altogether, as it did in the Scottish Highlands when a well or spring was wrongfully treated or desecrated in such a way. Certain other wells, when stones (usually of quartz) were thrown into them, would react by causing a powerful storm. Some of these activities may have been deliberately offensive; in other cases it was the belief that the casting of white quartz stones (fairy fire-stones, as they were called in Scotland) into the well would raise a storm and so bring rain.

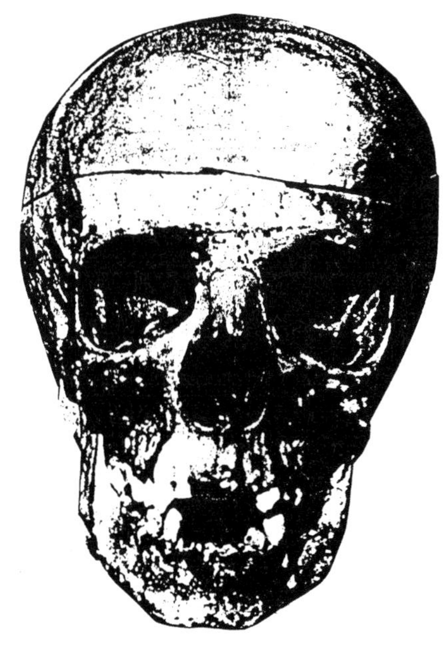

35a Saint Teilo's skull, Llandilo-isaf, Pembrokeshire. See A. Ross 1999, pl.4

The springs at Bath, Aquae Sulis, in Somerset were long famous for their healing qualities, which operated when the sacred water was drunk. It is full of unpleasant-tasting minerals, as I found to my cost when I drank a glass. A fascinating feature of these Romano-British springs, which must have been venerated long before Roman times under the aegis of their Celtic goddess Sulis, was the number of curse-tablets (*defixiones*) which were found at Aquae Sulis. None of these would seem to have been discovered in Wales, although some wells were used for malevolent purposes. There was no consistency in belief; for example *ffynnon y Cythraul*, 'Devil's well', had the reputation of being a normal well for healing. On the other hand, *ffynnon Pechod* (Anglesey) and *ffynnon Angau* (Carmarthenshire) may have had some sinister background. Nevertheless *ffynnon y Pasg* ('the Easter spring'), Denbighshire, would seem to have been solely associated with Christianity.

People who wished to curse their enemies were in the habit of throwing bent pins into the well. In my own tradition a pin, bent or straight, was a fertility symbol and pins were thrown into the waters in order to promote fertility. In Anglesey, *ffynnon Estyn* had a strange reputation. Formerly the water used to be carried to the baptismal font. In recent times the local people have been unwilling to drink from it, saying that it was once a cursing well.

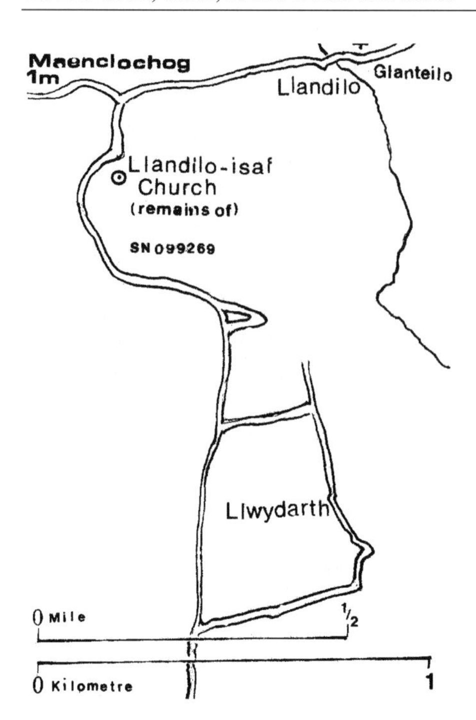

35b Location of the ruined church of Llandilo-Isaf

Ceiniogau corff was the name given to the pennies that had been employed to close the eyes of a dead person, and these would be thrown as offerings into the well as the water was drunk. It was believed that to drink the water from *ffynnon Fach* in Montgomery would be fatal, but that it was safe to bathe in it.

One well, *ffynnon Elian*, was an outstandingly evil well. It has been suggested that it was pre-Christian in origin. It began as a healing well and then, in the second part of the eighteenth century, it gained a reputation for the ability to punish people, and, more seriously, to kill them. There was a major attempt on the part of the authorities to try to suppress the use of the well for nefarious purposes, but it was fruitless. It cost one shilling to curse somebody, and ten shillings to remove the curse (*dad-offrum*). To take the curse off, the guardian had to empty the well and hand to the supplicant the slate bearing his name. The supplicant then returned home and had to read on three successive Fridays large portions of the Book of Job and the Psalms. The curse would then be removed. This well, about which so many legends accrued, was finally destroyed.

Charms for curing could also be used for healing at sacred or holy wells. For example, if one suffered from warts and wished to be free of them, there is a specific charm. It consisted of dropping a pin into a holy well and the result would be that the warts drop off or otherwise disappear. Should anyone, however, decide to remove the pin out of the well, the warts would immediately begin to grow again.

36 Llanbadarn Fawr, Ceredigion. The weather-worn cross shaft now within the church. Circa *tenth century*

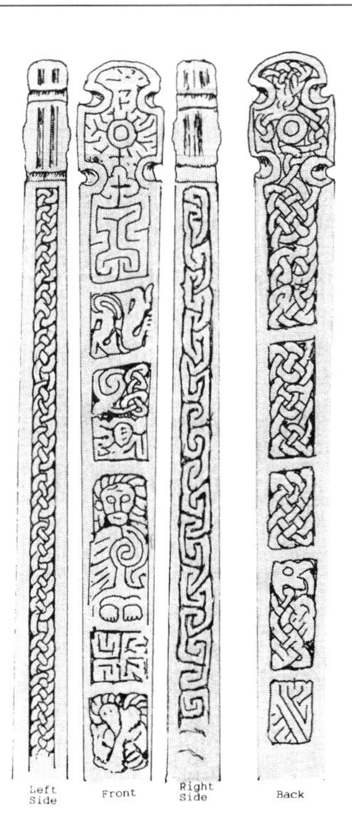

Llanbadarn Fawr (The Church of St Padarn the Great) (36)

The lives of the Welsh saints — as of those of Ireland — are a major source for folklore of the church, its saints and relics. They are too numerous to be dealt with in any detail in this book, but cannot altogether be omitted. As a member of St Padarn's Church at Llanbadarn Fawr, Ceredigion, it is understandable that I should wish to make some reference to our revered and colourful saint, his supposed origins and his legend.

Paternus or Padarn was seemingly born in Brittany. This is queried in for example *The Oxford Companion to the Literature of Wales* [*OCLW*]. Bartram, however, in his *Welsh Classical Dictionary* claims that he was born in Llydaw, i.e. Brittany.

A certain knight chanced to be passing in the vicinity of Llanbadarn in the early twelfth century on a feast day:

> When the clergy and the parishioners were awaiting the coming of their abbott, so that Mass could be celebrated, this knight was there to witness the abbott's arrival, in the midst of a crowd of other people. What he actually saw was a band of about 20 young men, all armed and equipped according to the local custom. He asked which was the abbott. They pointed out to him a man with a long spear in his hand, who was walking in front of the others. The knight gazed at him with amazement. 'Has the abbott no other vestments?' he

> asked. 'Has he no other staff to use instead of the spear which he is carrying?' 'No', they said. 'Upon my soul!' answered the knight. 'What I have seen today really is a novelty! I have never heard of anything so odd!' Without more ado he gave up travelling, put an end to his studies, and went straight back home.

This is followed by some strong imprecations which perhaps it is best not to repeat.

Cors Fochno (Borth Bog, Ceredigion)

This has long had a superstitious influence over those who traverse or live in proximity to it. It is, like Lindow Moss (*vide* Ross, *Druids*), a raised bog where peat-cutters used to report supernatural happenings and feelings. A pool on the edge of the bog is called *Pwll Du* (the Black Pool), believed to be bottomless and avoided by the local populace (it is now fenced in). A sinister hag was alleged to haunt the bog and should any peat-cutters steal her peat she would visit their homes at night and breathe sickness and disease over the family. Corpse candles were also frequently seen moving over the bog and it is generally regarded as a place to be avoided by the people.

Magical stones

An impressive stone near Kenfig, West Glamorgan, is known as Samson's Stone. According to local tradition, St Samson of Dôl, second Abbott of Caldey Island, threw this great monolith from Margam Mountain to its present site. It has at least one interesting legend associated with it although, doubtless, there are many other tales. The legend has it that before cock-crow on every Christmas morning it moves of its own volition and goes down to the nearby river Sker in order to drink. This is by no means a unique legend where standing stones are concerned, but it may be of interest to note that there is a very close parallel in Dorset near to the Iron Age hillfort of Pilsden Pen above Bettiscombe Manor where there is not only a screaming skull but a very large stone near the summit of the hill; this is alleged, every Christmas morning, to roll down to the pond beside the manor to drink. Numerous stones are widely believed to have powers of individual life and movement, and many have unusual legends attached to them.

A very strange and somewhat alarming rock is situated near Cross Inn, Ceredigion, and is known locally as Carreg y Big or Llech Bron. The top of the stone resembles a head. It is 14ft high and 9ft in diameter and having the appearance of a huge, monstrous being it would not be surprising if it were a

37 Pont ar Fynach, *Devil's Bridge, Ceredigion. The lowest is an earlier medieval bridge, said to have been built by the Devil. The next above is a later medieval bridge, said to have been built by the monks of Ystrad Fflur, Strata Florida. The uppermost bridge is a comparatively recent work of the County Council*

source of terror to a person coming upon it unexpectedly, especially in moonlight. There is a local legend that the present position of the stone was due to Satan who carried it from the summit of a rocky eminence known as Truchrug Mountain with the intention of using it in his work of building the very famous bridge, Devil's Bridge across the River Mynach (**37**). However the stone was too weighty even for him and he had to take a rest. After a while a cock suddenly crowed and the Devil leaped to his feet and disappeared, leaving the stone behind. It is alleged that his fingerprints may still be visible if one examines the stone closely.

The Devil was accredited with building several bridges, perhaps the most famous of which is that in Cardiganshire where there are now three intimidating bridges one above the other, across the rocky gorge. Many legends are told of this site. The Devil was seemingly entitled to the soul of the first person or animal to cross the bridge each day. There is a current legend which tells how the he was outwitted on one occasion.

Parc y Meirw, Llanlower, Fishguard, Pembrokeshire, has a remarkable row of eight huge stones which were erected at intervals over some 130ft. Only four of these now stand upright. It is a site which, being associated with *y meirw*, the dead, is even more prone to superstitious legends. One maintains that a white lady is sometimes seen in the vicinity of these monoliths. A ghostly woman in white is currently being seen some three miles from my home, standing beside the old stone archway which leads into the grounds of a mansion. I drove past recently late at night and although I did not see the ghost, there was an eerie atmosphere and I was glad to be on the road home!

Bryn yr Ellyllon (Hill of the Elves) near Mold, Clwyd has now been destroyed but it was the focus of a remarkable piece of Welsh folklore and archaeological discovery. Strangely enough, the story of the mound was first recounted to me by my teacher of Old Norse whilst doing my degrees at the University of Edinburgh. The story as he told it has since been substantiated and is a very interesting example of how folklore and archaeology can support and thus illuminate each other. The tale went that for many, many years the children of Mold were told that a certain mound contained the body of a nobleman, clad in golden armour and equipped with his weapons. This was widely believed to be true but the older people tended to scorn it. However, before the excavation had begun, a number of local people claimed that they had seen the spectre of a horseman with his horse clad in golden armour.

In 1833 the mound was excavated and many tons of stone were carted away and the skeleton of a very tall, well-built man was found stretched out in the grave. He had been interred wearing a superb corselet of gold which had been lined with bronze. This magnificent, elaborately ornamented object was thought to have been a gold peytral or breastplate for a pony but was subsequently identified as a ceremonial cape for a king or chieftain. Some 300 amber beads were found nearby, traces of an iron object, and an urn containing ashes had been placed some three yards from the skeleton. Before the mound was excavated the ghost of a mounted man had been seen, the horse fitted with golden armour. Oral tradition had kept this remarkable site and its legends alive until it was finally uncovered. It is clearly a site of first importance for both archaeologists and folklorists. This amazing discovery nicely testifies to the way in which legends belonging to the oral tradition which persist in one area or another down the ages can suddenly attain veracity by archaeological or other excavation processes.

South of Cader Idris, Dolgellau, Gwynedd, some huge coffins were found, containing skeletons of very tall men: the Tall Men of Tal-y-Llyn, which were apparently discovered in 1684, near the lake. Hazel rods were beside them and this would seem to indicate that these men were possibly Druids. Hazel was a tree sacred to the Druids and the nuts were supposed to confer wisdom and knowledge of the Otherworld to those who obtained these fruits from a sacred tree. Cormac, Bishop of Cashel in Ireland in the ninth century, states that such rods used to be kept in the burial-place of the pagans, and that people regarded it as an honour to touch these things. It was also said that the pagans used to write on such sticks in the Ogam script (*vide* Ross, *Druids*). Several deposits of a votive nature and of great importance to the history of Celtic toreutic art were found at Tal-y-Llyn, including fragments of a bronze shield-mount, tankard handles and other articles.

Din Lligwy, on the east side of Anglesey (Môn), consists of a group of *circa* fourth-century hut circles surrounded by a walled enclosure. Here in the immediately post-Roman period, parties of Irish invaders (Gwyddyl) settled in Anglesey and created stone-walled strongholds for defence purposes. Anglesey was probably one, if not the most, important druidic centre in Britain and it formed an invaluable point of contact linking it with both Ireland and the Welsh mainland. The great hoard of treasure found during hasty excavations carried out by Sir Cyril Fox in 1942 whilst the Valley airfield was being constructed can only be some indication of the lavish nature of what we must consider to have been votive deposits, made at a time when the Romans were pushing relentlessly northwards and both British and Irish independence was under threat. The votive nature of the site of the deposition, at Llyn Cerrig Bach near Holyhead, was emphasised by the fact that many of the weapons and other articles had been deliberately broken in a manner which archaeologists recognise to signify offerings. In other words these valuable items of weapons of various kinds would seem to have been 'decommissioned' as it were — thus ensuring that an offering could not thereafter be found and reused for secular purposes. Amongst the treasures were some Irish iron slave-chains and other metalwork from Ireland. Other fragments showed that similar items had been deposited from other areas of Britain, including Yorkshire. This would suggest that here we have a united British and Irish attempt to stem the ruthless northward thrust of the enemy. As we know from later history, these efforts were sadly in vain.

There was no time to collect and analyse the bones or to extend the work over a wider area. It is miraculous that Sir Cyril was able to retrieve so much, literally from the jaws of the great bulldozers. It may be remarked that it was about this time that the bodies of two high-born men and a woman whose head alone has to date been recovered must have been deposited in the lake on Lindow Moss, Cheshire. It is not impossible that the three had been chosen from the druidic order at a time of utterly dire need when the

38 One of the Bronze Age megaliths embedded in the churchyard wall at Ysbyty Cynfyn, Ceredigion

Romans were steadily lessening the distance between themselves and these, some of the last freedom fighters. Much can be conjectured just as further supportive evidence may come to light in the future.

It was good psychology on the part of the early Christians to seek to control the dark powers of the great Neolithic slabs of stone, scattered widely throughout the British Isles, sometimes singly and often in rows and circles. In general these are outside the scope of our enquiry. Nevertheless, much folklore has and does adhere to them. They sometimes occur as rings or groups of three or other numbers and it was often a tradition to incorporate these pagan monuments into the hallowed walls of the Christian churchyard and so control any evil powers which might still be retained by them. Perhaps one of the finest examples of these monuments is to be found close to Devil's Bridge in Dyfed at a site called Ysbyty Cynfyn (**38**). It is a most impressive sight: the pagan stones standing upright at regular intervals in the churchyard wall and the old church keeping a very watchful eye on them. One is reminded very much of the instructions of Pope Gregory I (the Great) to St Augustine *c.*AD 590 concerning his mission to convert the pagan Anglo-Saxons. He told him to 'destroy the idols but to leave the structures intact; to allow the people to come to worship there but not to honour the old gods but the Lord God Almighty; at their festival seasons to allow the people to bring their animals to the church but to slaughter them under the aegis of Christianity and not of their heathen deities'. This little church of Ysbyty Cynfyn has a peculiar sense of power despite its physical insignificance in the midst of vast areas of wild countryside.

St Gofan's Well

This small well contained in a simple stone structure is directly below the chapel of St Gofan, south of Pembroke (**39**). Situated close to the attractive little building, the well is built in a narrow gap in the cliffs which are, like the surrounding landscape, of limestone. The well has been allowed to dry

39 St Gofan's chapel, Pembrokeshire

up but in the past it was very important as a curative well. People suffering from leg and foot diseases would travel long distances to seek the cure. This consisted, no doubt, of the repetition of some incantation or prohibition and the bathing of the afflicted part in the sacred water. Many claimed to have been cured, and as a token of their healing, they would leave their crutches behind them.

7 Giants, water monsters and inhabitants of the Otherworld

Taliesin

Tradition suggests that Taliesin lived at the same time as the great poets Aneurin, Talhaearn Tad Awen, and others, all of whom flourished in or around the sixth century AD. The Book of Taliesin was copied from a manuscript probably dating to the late thirteenth century. The original manuscript was written in Old Welsh somewhere between the sixth and seventh centuries AD.

The tradition of the birth of Taliesin (known as *Hanes Taliesin*) is one of the great stories of the Welsh. The earliest full version of the tale dates to the sixteenth century. There is evidence to show that different versions of it existed long before that date. The story is remarkably similar in theme to the Irish story of how the hero Fionn obtained his prophetic knowledge. When he was a young boy, Taliesin was known as Gwion Bach (Gwion equates linguistically with the Irish Fionn; Gw in Welsh being equal to F in Irish). The boy Taliesin was hired by the lake goddess Ceridwen, who lived under Bala Lake with her husband, Tegid, after whom the lake was named in Welsh — Llyn Tegid. The source of the River Dyfrdwy (Dee) is in this lake. In a well-known Celtic motif, i.e. the cauldron of inspiration, Ceridwen was brewing up poetic inspiration in it for nearly a year and the boy Taliesin was to help her by watching it closely and making sure that no one should taste one single drop of the mysterious brew. One day, some liquid was inadvertently spilt and three drops fell onto the boy's finger. Immediately he was able to have foreknowledge of all that was about to happen. He realised that Ceridwen was his enemy and her intention was to kill him as soon as he had completed his duty of guarding the magical brew. He knew that he must escape from her with all speed. This he attempted to carry out and every time Ceridwen was catching up with him he turned himself into a variety of different forms but she always thwarted him. Eventually, seeing some wheat on the ground, he turned himself into a grain of the cereal but Ceridwen instantly changed herself into a hen and swallowed him. After the necessary lapse of time, he was reborn from her womb as a beautiful child. Such was his beauty that the goddess, his mother, could not bear to kill him. Instead she wrapped him up in the hide of an animal and cast him out to sea. The hide containing the baby was recovered at Aberdovey on the first of May, a portentous season for magic. At that time a man named Elphyn went with his men to the weir where the hide had been caught up. Thinking it might contain riches, he asked his servant to look inside it where, to his astonishment, he saw the top of a baby's forehead (*tal iessin*) so Elphyn said the boy should be called Taliesin and lifted him up in his arms. The baby immediately sang a poem in order to console Elphyn who had hoped the hide contained gold. Shortly afterwards he sang two more poems which were answers to questions about his former existence and as to his amazing knowledge. This motif is known in other Celtic contexts and there are of course variations in the details of the story, which must have had a long oral tradition behind it. And so the boy lived and grew to become one of the most famous poets in all Wales. This whole story of course is suggestive of druidism with its powerful belief in metempsychosis and immortality.

The *afanc* (water monster)

The *afanc* is a terrifying water monster which figures in medieval and later Welsh tradition. There is hardly a lake or pool in Wales without its legend. The legendary horned oxen of Hu Gadarn were the means by which the lake *afanc* was dragged to dry land so that the lake did not burst afterwards. In many ways the *afanc* — which is thought to be some kind of supernatural beaver or other water creature — resembles the Gaelic *each uisge* which, although invariably appearing in horse form, comes to land in the shape of a handsome youth when in search of a young girl to drag back into its watery lair; and — unless she is very lucky — devour her. In one instance, at least, the *afanc* takes on this rôle.

There is a pool on the Conwy River, known as Llyn yr Afanc. A young — and we should think foolish — girl enticed the monster to come out of the pool. She obviously accepted his amorous advances and the creature fell asleep, his head resting on her knees, and his claws grasping one of her breasts. He was bound with chains during his deep slumber. When he woke up and saw the chains he made straight for the pool, the girl's breast still in his claws. Although bound with chains, he managed to return to the pool but part of the chain was long enough for those lying in wait to fasten to the horned oxen, who dragged the *afanc* back to land. A pass which the *afanc* and the oxen traversed is, according to T. Gwynn Jones, still known as *Bwlch Rhiw'r Ychen* (the pass in the hill of the oxen). Likewise, the moor where one of the oxen lost an eye is called *Gweun Llygad Ych* (the moor of the ox's eye) and *Pwll Llygad Ych* is 'the pool of the ox's eye'. The poor animals dragged the *afanc* right up to *Llyn Cwm Ffynnon Las*, 'the lake of the hollow of the blue spring'. A not dissimilar tale seems to have been known in connection with Llyn Barfog, near Aberdovey, but the *afanc* was dragged out by King Arthur and his war-horses.

There is a whole world of traditions concerning waters, pools, lakes and certainly rivers, which may indicate the deep-rooted Celtic feeling for such features. This is certainly the case in Gaelic Scotland as it is in Ireland, and no doubt widely throughout Europe. Rivers are fascinating and sometimes intimidating permanent elements of the landscape, and hundreds of tales must once have been — and in some places still are — recited or read about in books. They are ever-changing and man must always have had an uneasy relationship with them.

Giants

Belief in people of abnormal height known as giants exists in most parts of the world. There are human beings who certainly attain to a height and girth which is markedly greater than the average human stature, but these are not usually regarded as giants nor are they thought to possess the supernatural powers which are common to the giants of folklore. Wales is extremely rich in its repertoire of giant legends, which are widespread and do not always concur with our own ideas of gigantology. They have a well-known place in the folklore of the British Isles and on the whole they would seem to be virtually harmless in non-aggressive contexts. They are by no means lacking in intelligence, if their legends are to be accepted as truth. The subject is too large for a major investigation of the phenomena here and I propose simply to consider half a dozen or so of the more impressive examples.

I myself live some three miles from an imposing 'giant' to whom a legend is still attached, on land which belonged to the Gogerddan Estate. Plas Gogerddan was owned by the Prys family who possessed the stretch of flat lands (the Bow Street Flats) which lie on the left of the main road to Aberystwyth and which have in recent years been subjected to a considerable amount of examination and archaeological excavation. Here stands the great giant Cerdden, who originally formed part of a Neolithic circle of standing stones, two of which remain, the more imposing being regarded as a representation of Cerddan Cawr, 'Cerddan the Giant', who is sometimes referred to as Erddan. His home was connected with a hillfort behind the Bow Street Flats. The two standing stones that represent the remains of the original circle are giants who were enemies and used to periodically fight with one another, according to tradition. There is a legend amongst the local people that the grave of a giant exists at either end of the Flats. Excavation in the past few years has revealed traces of a Neolithic burial ground on the Bow Street Flats and the imposing figure of the remaining standing stone known as Cerddan Cawr — said to have fought triumphantly against a second giant. There is another Cerddan giant in Montgomeryshire who fought against the giant Iestyn.

Welsh toponomy is rich in giants' and giantesses' names, beings which seem to have held a particular fascination for the Welsh, although are by no means lacking in Irish mythology. St Patrick comments on the huge size of the resuscitated Irish warriors in comparison with their own stature. Arthur was a giant, one of many in Wales.

Mermaids and mermen

These strnge beings were believed to inhabit the seacoasts of Wales and could be dangerous to the local people. The Welsh mermaid does not differ fundamentally from the universal concept. Down to her waist she is described as a young woman of great beauty. Below the waist she resembles a fish, having fins and a typical fish tail. Male sea creatures were called mermen and both sexes had long hair which they constantly combed with great vanity. The mermaids could sing sweet songs with which they, siren-like, could lure people to their deaths. It was a strong belief that the great beauty of the mermaid could induce handsome young men to fall in love with them and they would often entice these eager suitors to their watery dwellings at the bottom of the sea. Elias Owen mentions a story he believes he heard in Caernarfonshire, p.142f. It is typical of many such tales. The legend notes that a man caught a mermaid and took her back to his home and the poor creature continuously begged to be allowed to return to the sea, but her captor kept her in a room and fastened the door securely. She lasted for a few days, constantly pleading for her release, which was denied her and so she died. From then on, the man who had imprisoned her seemed to have been cursed. He went from bad to worse and finally died in great poverty. It was widely held that it was very unlucky to harm these marine beings. People believed in those days that any cruelty would result in severe punishment to the perpetrator.

Many Welsh traditions, some of a great age, were concerned with a supernatural woman, perhaps a water deity, who lived under a lake or in various watery places. One such story, recorded by Elias Owen, is entitled the *Myddfai Legend*. The story begins with the well-known theme, the widow who has an only son. Here, she possesses large flocks of cattle, some of which she must get her son to drive to graze on the Black Mountain. Nearby was a small lake called Llyn y Fan Fâch (**40**).

One day, the son perceived, to his amazement, a very lovely young woman with long, flowing hair, who was sitting on the calm surface of the lake, and, using the water as a looking-glass, combing her locks. He persuaded her to

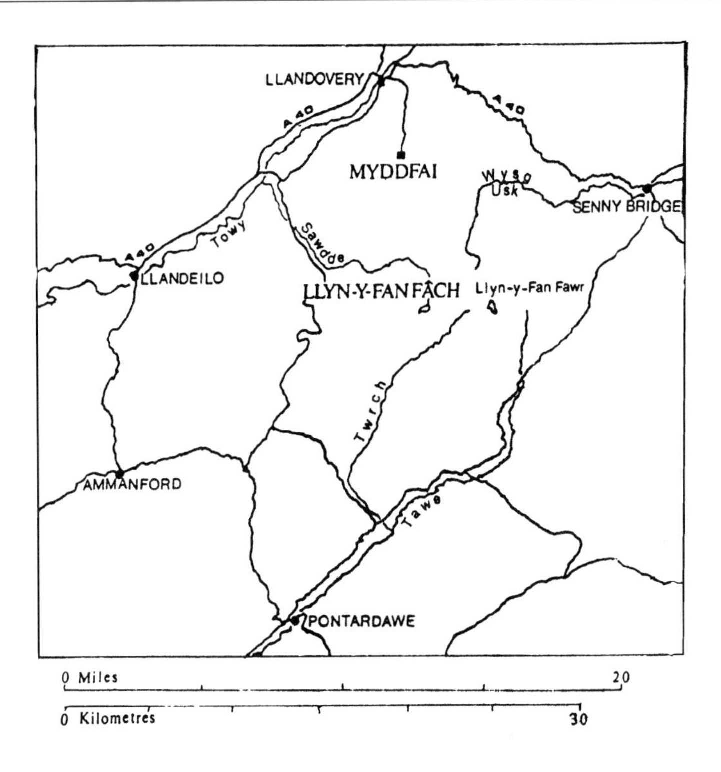

40 Myddfai and Llyn-y-Fan Fâch, Carmarthenshire

become his wife and she consented, making however one condition, namely that they should live together until he gave her three undeserved blows. If that were to happen she would leave him for ever. He accepted these conditions instantly and was filled with joy. Thus the lake lady gave her hand to the young man. The young couple were then married and went to live at a farm called Esgair Llaethdy, near Myddfai. There they lived in prosperity and happiness for several years and became the parents of three fine sons. But the first two of the causeless blows had been dealt. Years passed, their children had grown up, and were three outstandingly clever young men. Surrounded by so many worldly blessings, the husband forgot that only one causeless blow would destroy his prosperity. He was very careful in case any trivial happening should occur, that his wife would regard as a breach of their marriage contract. She told him that she loved him as much as ever, and warned him to be careful in case, through carelessness, he might give her the last of the three blows, which if it happened, would separate them for ever. However the last blow was eventually struck and she left, never to be seen by her husband again. This legend is recounted in full in chapter 9 *infra*.

The torrent spectre

Many mountain torrents and high streams (**front cover**) were believed to be haunted by, or be the dwelling-place of, fierce spectres or other malevolent spirits bearing names which we shall meet with in other parts of this work. The spectre in question was conceived as being in the form of an old man or an evil spirit who was ruler of the mountain torrents, controlling the waters and the events connected with them. It was his great joy to see the lands flooded and revel in the chaos and human distress which such events occasioned. He was a terrifying creature to chance upon and it was widely believed that the outline of his frightening shape could actually be glimpsed beneath the water, seemingly moving forward with the rushing waters but in fact remaining stationary. Sometimes he would rise up half out of the water and then ascend to a considerable height, equal to at least half the height of the highest mountain. He resembled one of the frightening mists that one experiences in the Scottish Highlands as well as in Wales, a mist that takes on changing forms and resembles a variety of monstrous beings, semi-human or semi-animal. Later he would shrink until he was the size of a man. He had a savage countenance and an even more disturbing laugh. He had long hair which stood on end and was constantly enshrouded by mist. Right up to the nineteenth century, and possibly beyond, there were those who had complete belief in this alarming creature in both Glamorganshire and Radnorshire.

Another fearsome water-creature was the female known as *Gwrach y Rhibyn* (hag of the mist). Her dwelling was supposed to be in dense fog: thus she was rarely glimpsed. She used to utter a hideous shriek, believed by the local people to portend some misfortune or indeed death itself. Some nervous inhabitants of the region thought that she would shriek out the name of one who was soon to die. Another aspect of this horror was known as *yr Hen Chrwchwd* (the old hump-backed one) which was in fact a fiend in the form of an old woman and believed to be the same demon as *Gwrach y Rhibyn*. In Carmarthenshire this monster of the mist is not described as an old woman but as a white-haired old man who sits on the point of the hill where the clouds rest. He is known as the Grey King, *y Brenhin Llwyd*. He may have controlled the movements of the mist but his function is not entirely clear.

The water horse

The concept of the mythological animal in the form of a horse known in Scotland as the 'kelpie' or *each-uisge*, in Wales as *ceffyl y dwr*, is common to all the Celtic countries. He was widely believed to be a malevolent spirit who took on the shape of a horse and tried to make people get on his back, whereupon he would swim out into the water and attempt to drown them. He could take on the form of a very handsome and desirable young man who would lure attractive girls in order to ravish them and then bring about their watery end. Sometimes, as in the Highlands of Scotland, he would still have waterweed clinging to his hair and traces of hooves were still present about his feet. Lucky girls could note these dread signs and, lulling him to sleep by their sweet singing, could creep away and run for their lives, praying he would not wake up and follow them.

The water-horse of Wales, *ceffyl y dwr*, bore a marked similarity to his Gaelic counterpart. It was seemingly a belief in Wales that the clergy could ride on the back of a water-horse without incurring any danger. There is one tale of a clergyman who was riding a *ceffyl y dwr* while his parish clerk accompanied them on foot. The priest felt sorry for him and invited him to get up behind him, on the understanding that he would not speak while they were riding the animal, and so they proceeded for a while and the parish clerk did not utter a word. The horse went at a lively pace and, noting this, the clerk exclaimed aloud, and was immediately thrown to the ground. The priest remained where he was and, leaving the clerk on the ground, reviled him for not keeping his tongue quiet.

Motley comments that the *ceffyl y dwr* was widely believed to be an evil spirit who could take on the form of a horse and approach the unsuspecting traveller or stranger with an invitation to get on his back. When he did so, the horse would either rise up into the air, or gallop over rivers and mountains, suddenly disappearing into the mist while throwing the rider to certain death. He is identical with the kelpie of Scottish tradition and the phoocah (*púca*) of the Irish.

It was believed that the water-horses did not always remain in lakes and rivers, but would exercise themselves on the hills and play with the small native ponies before they became a mixed breed. Certain people, who knew the correct procedure, could call up a water-horse by means of shaking a magical bridle over the pool which it inhabited.

The monster of Llyn Tegid, Bala, Gwynedd

The monster has been sighted at regular intervals since *c.*1967 and the descriptions given by witnesses are remarkably similar. He has been nicknamed Anghenfil for some reason or another. A sighting is recorded for 1983 when a man, gazing down at the lake one morning, was astounded to see a strange object some 10ft in length progressing in a leisurely fashion towards the bank. He ran down to the shore but there was no sign of the monster. A fuller description of the creature was given by a local man who was fishing at the edge of the lake. The creature rose up and made in his direction. Its body was about 8ft in length, its skin dark and slimy and it had a very large head with malevolent eyes. It remained on the surface for some short while and then plunged back into the water.

The Mawddach monster

This monster allegedly lives in the Mawddach Estuary, Barmouth, Gwynedd. Sightings of it have been recorded for many years and a great number of people have alleged that they have seen it. It is described as having 'a long neck, a square face and a long tail with a flipper at the back, and its skin was black and patchy'. A local woman claimed that she had seen four large footprints ('as big as an elephant's') in the sand near Barmouth. Yet another sighting was reported by one Mr Jones of Harlech in 1937 who noticed a 'crocodile-like creature' walking along a riverbank immediately outside the town. A shopkeeper mounted a display of newspaper cuttings about the sightings of the monster. Nothing further seems to have been recorded about this strange creature.

Conclusion

Monsters have always been a source of fascination and, at a time when people still believed in them and were convinced that they had come face to face with them, they must have been a constant cause for apprehension. Monster tales survived even if the monsters — real or imaginary — did not, and they continue to intrigue us today. Perhaps we need monsters, or think we do. This is suggested by, for example, the most enigmatic and longed-for monster, known as the Loch Ness monster, which allegedly lurks in the seemingly bottomless waters of Loch Ness, in Inverness-shire, Scotland. From time to time 'sightings' have been made of this widely famed beast and there is some convincing evidence for its existence in the so-called 'Dark Ages'. The earliest records of sightings occur in the *Vita Sanctae Columbae* (*Life of St Columba*), when the saint, on a journey from Iona to Inverness to try to Christianise the pagan Pictish king, Brude, saw one of his followers being seized and almost swallowed by the bloodthirsty beast. He cursed it and restored the young cleric to life but it was an uncomfortable moment. The fame of the monster has never diminished and has become virtually worldwide but it has been to date impossible to verify the various sightings recorded down the ages.

Similar monsters are associated with lakes and rivers throughout the world and there seems to be a deep psychological need in mankind for these obnoxious animals. The possibility of recreating dinosaurs from their DNA is currently being considered. Personally, I do not think the reality would be very comfortable, and that those who endured dinosaurs would have been very relieved to see them eradicated. However, the search for monsters goes on, and there are quite a few of these reputed to lurk in Welsh waters, as we have seen.

The traditions of Eryri

Llyn Dinas

I am indebted to my friend John E. Williams of Llanrug, Gwynedd, for this story.

When Myrddin Emrys had built a castle for Gwrtheyrn Gwrthenau, the king ascended the turrets and from that elevation he beheld two dragons fighting in the lake, namely the red dragon and the white dragon. After watching them for a while furiously battling with each other, he called to Myrddin the Druid and asked him what was going on. Myrddin — well-versed in the mysticism and secretive wizardry of all the ages — prophesied what emblem there would be for the nation of the Cymry (the Welsh) or the British for the long centuries ahead (*see* **16**). The red dragon belonged to the nation of the Cymry and the white dragon symbolised the English nation. The two dragons had been hidden for many ages past by the deity Llydd ap Beli in the stronghold of Affaraon in the rocks of Eryri (Snowdonia). It was in the time of Gwrtheyrn that the dragons' lair was revealed. Nennius says that Myrddin explained the mystery of the dragons and other historians say that the dragons killed each other and that their blood was so copious and flowed so abundantly that it turned the waters of the lake red.

The local belief is that the dragon seen first in the lake was peaceful and harmless but after the dreadful battle it almost destroyed the other dragon, diving after it to the bottom of the lake; eventually it rose to the surface dragging the body of its enemy on its back, the blood having coloured it bright red. However, despite its horrific wounds it survived, and that is how Pendragon became the *cyfenw* (title) of the Welsh princes, especially those who overcame their enemies in battle.

8 Omens, second sight and seers

General death omens

Omens of death and disaster were very widespread, particularly in the Celtic countries, where these would seem to have been slightly more detailed and in which birds played a singular rôle. A belief concerning the 'death bird' (*aderyn corff*) in the form of a domestic fowl was the crowing of a cock in the night. The crowing itself was sinister and at once it was necessary for whoever heard it to find out the position the bird's head was in while crowing. When its head was turned away from that person's home and faced somebody else's house, the occupants would return to sleep in the belief that it was a neighbour and not one of their own family who was about to die.

There were various sounds which warned of approaching death. These varied from shrieking to a tapping or knocking sound, and included the following. For example there was the *cyhyraeth*, made by a plaintive spirit. The noise was alarming enough to make the hair of the head rise and those who heard it would turn icy cold. It was quite unearthly and very distinctive. There was nothing to be seen but plenty to be heard, to such an extent that dogs would cower and run into some hiding place.

Another death portent was that of an unnatural knocking, especially the noise of a joiner preparing a coffin for the deceased. This is a very widespread motif in the British Isles. Owls, solitary crows, geese and hens in certain situations and positions could be warnings of imminent death and there seems to have been no limit to the ways in which the superstitious mind could be thus disturbed, to the strong disapproval of the Church which abhorred all such heathen beliefs.

The corpse candle (*cannwyll corff*)

Elias Owen seems to have collected much of his oral tradition himself at a time when such traditions were still very much alive, in the late nineteenth century. Some of the material he published is relatively unknown and a certain proportion had already been published in the same or similar form in various books or journals. The concept of the corpse candle is very widespread in the Celtic countries, and there is little variation in the basic tale. After dark, someone leaves his home to carry out a task in the yard, byre or some other part of the property and he, or perhaps she, notices a light some distance away in a place where there is no building whatsoever. At first this arouses the onlooker's interest, but gradually this is supplanted by an ever-increasing fear and the feeling that the steady progression of this light is by no means a good omen. When the observer sees the light drawing ever closer to his own property, he is filled with a terrible fear and recognises its ominous character. Invariably he makes for the house and, rushing indoors, shuts the door tight and turns to secure it; as he does so, he sees to his infinite dismay that the light has come through the closed door and is making its way up the stairs of the dwelling. He knows that this is the unequivocal sign that there is to be a death in the house that night. All seems to be well and, not having communicated the vision to any member of his family, but — fearing the worst — he retires to bed and the house is quiet. Next morning, a servant, a member of the family or the man himself is found dead in bed. The corpse candle has done its work. I myself have heard many stories of people in other parts of Britain who have — in order to reach their homes — had to cross tracks over treacherous bogland. The corpse candle is often reported as having been seen by these travellers but to date I have heard no account of these apparitions ending in death.

Sometimes a more mundane reason lies at the root of the spectral light and its movements. It was a custom, before electric torches were invented, to place a home-made candle (made from melted mutton fat with the wick from rushes dipped in it and allowed to harden) in a jar and sometimes a moving light would be seen crossing the darkness of the peat bog. As it drew nearer, the person walking towards it would be increasingly unnerved, mistaking the light for a corpse candle. When it became clear that the bearer of the light was a neighbour or even a stranger the sense of relief must have been enormous. There are, of course, natural bog phenomena which resemble moving lights, known in England and Scotland as Will o' the Wisp. I have heard many tales of these from my mother; she, my young daughter and I have witnessed this very phenomenon near Aberfoyle in Perthshire. The manifestation is well described in the very useful *Daily Express Encyclopedia* (Volume 8) thus:

> Will o' the wisp, properly called *Ignis fatuus*, is a pale flickering flame sometimes seen over marshes. It is generally assumed to be due to marsh gas produced by decaying vegetable, and possibly also animal, material spontaneously igniting. It has given rise to much superstition, which is reflected in the name, and also in its alternative name, Jack-o'-Lantern.

Another name for this phenomenon in Wales is given by E. Owen as *Yr Ellyll Dân*, which he (writing at the end of the nineteenth century) comments is the common name for *Ignis fatuus*. Fairies, or the Fair Family, as they were sometimes called, were often associated with marshy or rushy places of the kind we have been considering.

Motley describes the *cannwyl corff* in a different way, regarding it perhaps as a kind of animal with an independent existence. He notes that this 'animal', or 'Will o' the Wisp' as he describes it, tricked any lost travellers to leave the safe path and lured them to their doom in terrible peat bogs or quagmires, by these

> 'Flying phantoms' which are generally believed by the ignorant to be evil spirits. Some years ago, the form, face, and wings of the 'animal' said to be the nucleus of this light, were circumstantially described in a short paper in the Mirror, which seem to bear the marks of implicit faith on the part of the narrator.

Motley states that he has frequently seen the *cannwyl corff*, not only moving over the bogs but also upon the mountain roads of Glamorganshire, seemingly adapting its pace to that of his horse. He notes that the light has an unfortunate tendency to leave the comparative safety of the track and to venture onto the dangerous bog-land, filling the unwary traveller with an overpowering desire to follow it; this inevitably leads to tragedy. Motley himself records that he once witnessed a particular aspect of this 'evil' light, apparently during the cold weather of January 1842 when he was riding across a mountain road near Maesteg. This time the horseman's boots and the fetlocks of the horse seemed to blaze with a blue light and when the rider's hand was stretched out every finger at once became tipped with fire. He also states that these appearances are called in Welsh *ellyl dân* or goblin fire. In Glamorganshire, according to Motley, there is a small valley which was said to be widely known for the brightness and the frequency of such appearances, which have caused it to gain the reputation of being haunted by spirits of an even darker nature. On account of this, the valley in question is named the Valley of Spirits. Motley quotes one Allies as reporting that some of the ghostly lights of the Welsh bog-lands were able to point out to travellers the right path across them but goes on to comment: 'but of these I have never heard'.

Divination (*dewiniaeth*, *rhamanta* or *difaliaeth*)

The Celts as an ancient and widely-scattered people have preserved many archaic tendencies, customs and beliefs. Superstition and second sight, as well as deliberate omen-seeking, have always been a feature of their spiritual proclivities and superstitious practice. The word *rhamanta* is an archaic word; it would be more usual to call it *dewiniaeth* or *difaliaeth*, meaning divination or omen-seeking. It was a special kind of divination, which could be carried out alone by the one seeking to ascertain what would happen to him or her or those related to the would-be diviner, without the intercession of any other person. Neither Druids nor their successors or witches or any other such 'disreputable' persons had any rôle to play in this archaic process of *rhamanta*. We shall look at a few examples of this practice as recorded once again in the invaluable work of Elias Owen, whose religious calling did not prejudice him against an objective study of what he might well regard as pagan practices.

The examples which have been published in various books are very numerous and there are still oral traditions current which show that all memory of divination in this way has not been lost. It must have been somewhat alarming to go to the prescribed place where the future could be revealed or to participate in the necessary ritual, even in one's home — one could surely never be certain what supernatural forces were being released to the detriment of the seeker after future knowledge. This being the case, rather than one young girl setting out for any given point on her own, the tendency was for, say, three to go together to keep each other company and to assist each other should the situation become too frightening or the revelations too distressing for a single person to handle. But it has always been the way with young single people to try to divine if and whom they were to marry and they placed what might be regarded as a totally misguided faith in these omens. To add to the general recklessness of such 'seeking', it was generally carried out in darkest night and, at midnight, they would start to chant the necessary or the relevant incantations. Sometimes the procedure was totally innocent; sometimes cruel practices were resorted to. One of them at least should have slept on a bed made of oat straw or one made from leaves of the rowan tree mixed with seeds of fern and with a pillow of the maidenhair variety.

There were special nights (the 'spirit nights') when omens and divination were particularly effective — Hallowe'en, or All Hallows Eve, as it is also known (*Nos Calan Gaeaf*) ; St John's Eve (*Nos Wyl Ifan*) and Mayday Eve (*Nos Calan Haf*) . These were three 'Spirit Nights' (*Ysbryd Nosau*). Of course, reading the omens where there was any doubt whatsoever about the manifestations, such as the direction in which the trail of a snail went, would immediately lead to whatever conclusion was desired. It would be more than easy to trace the name of the desired lover or beloved in the meanderings of the innocent mollusc. On St John's Eve, at midnight, young women customarily sought for the plant *Llysiau Ifan* — St John's wort — and the light of the glow-worm was believed to be helpful in this search. So this soft-bodied beetle must first be tracked down. When one was found, it would be carried in the palm of the hand and the desired plant sought amongst the fern-fronds. When sufficient had been collected, the flowers were made into a bouquet and carried to the girl's bedroom. If in the morning the leaves had not wilted, it was a sign that the desired one and the occupant of the bedroom would be married within a year. If however the leaves were found hanging down or dead, this portended the girl's own death or, alternatively, that she was not to get a husband within the year.

The Rev. Owen heard some oral traditions about the *rhamanta* and how one woman, who was still alive when he wrote in 1886, saw her future husband by *rhamanta* or divination, and her friend, also a servant, did likewise. Owen then relates a story that he had from oral sources. In outline, it was as follows: the young women in the rural areas of Wales were desperate to obtain a sight of the one they were destined to marry — no doubt some of them did not succeed in marrying at all. The mistress was let into the secret which was that same night that one of the two girls was going to try to look into the future and the second girl would do so the following night. The clock struck midnight and the second girl herself began to strike the floor with a leather strap, repeating the lines *Am gyd-fydio i gyd-ffatio*, or 'we live together to strike together', and immediately her master came down the stairs. Next day, the girl in all innocence questioned her mistress about her reason for sending her husband down the stairs to give her a fright. The mistress answered: 'Take care of my children'. In due course this girl married her master and it is clear that sadly, the girl's innocent question to her mistress had informed her of her own impending death. To return to the other girl, she saw a dark man but he was a stranger to her. However, only a week or two passed before a stranger walked into the farmyard and she at once recognised him as the person whom her divinations had revealed to her. Upon asking around the community, she discovered that he, too, was a married man. However, in due course his wife died and the servant girl became his second bride.

As young girls were so desperate not only to know that they would marry, but to discover who the man should be, they were much occupied in trying to discover this by occult means. One of these methods involved the aid of a ball of yarn. This mode of looking into the future was usually carried out at night by two young girls after all the other members of the household had gone to bed. It has been called *coel ede wlan* (let the wool reveal the future, or 'the yarn test'). It was carried out in this manner: two young women took hold of a ball of yarn and, using small pieces of wood, fashioned a miniature rope ladder. They then retired upstairs, opened a window, threw the artificial ladder down to the ground, and the girl who was carrying out the incantation began winding the ladder up, saying: '*Y fi sy'n dirwyn, Pwy sy'n dal?*' ('I am winding, who is holding?'). This was performed three times and, should no lover make his appearance, there would be no marriage that year. Next night the other girl tried to ascertain her future status, and with whom, and she hoped for better luck for her efforts. The belief was that the spirit of the future husband would mount the wool ladder and make himself known to his future wife.

Owen also records another tale which he collected orally from a fellow churchman, the Rev. R. Jones, rector of Llanycil. Two young men from Ffestiniog went off to court two girls in the parish of Maentwrog, who were employed as servants at a farm called Gellidywyll. As they were going towards the farm, one of them said 'I want to rest for a little'. He sat on the ground and seemed to fall asleep at once. This startled his friend, but he was terrified when he saw a blue light coming from his mouth. He tried to wake him up but could not arouse him; he appeared to be dead. However, after a time the blue light was seen returning, and it re-entered the mouth of the sleeping youth who instantly woke up, and they went on together towards Gellidywyll. It happened that at the very moment that he felt himself falling asleep, his love had used the yarn incantation, and during his short sleep, he dreamed that he had seen his sweetheart at her window, and the girl said that he had appeared at her window. In a few months the two were married.

Another form of divination was to walk around the church seven times or nine times on certain nights. Owen calls this the *twca* test, or knife test. He says that it was a very common method of incantation. This is how it went — the person who wished to know whom he or she would marry went secretly to the church and circumambulated it seven times, while repeating the following: '*Dyma'r twca, Lle mae'r wain*?' or 'Here's the knife, where's the sheath?' It was thought that the spirit of his or her future partner would become visible to the one who held the knife, with the sheath in his or her hand, and it would be found that the one fitted the other exactly. Owen comments that he was told by someone who made this test that if the person was to become a wife, the lover would surely appear to her; if it was her fate to die unmarried, then a coffin would come to meet her.

Another mode of seeing one's future partner was the washing test. In this form of divination the young woman had to take a garment to be washed, for example a stocking, to the water-spout or *pistyll*, and to carry two pieces of wood with which she would strike the garment being washed. She went on her knees and began to strike the stocking, saying '*Am gyd-fydio i gyd-ffatio*'. It was thought that her future husband would then appear, take up the second piece and join her in her work of beating. If the vision were to appear, then the marriage would take place within six months.

9 Folk healing, herbal remedies and charms

The Celts in general seem always to have had a partiality for and expertise in healing. Folk medicine often chanced upon truths that subsequent generations found it extremely difficult to better. Much ancient medical lore must have been lost in the early periods of our dependency on government from Rome. Yet it undoubtedly remained at a folk level, the ancient recipes for healing being handed on from generation to generation in the old manner. As early as the Neolithic period in European prehistory the art of trepanning was known and there is clear evidence for the long survival of many who had undergone this delicate operation, attested by bone growth in the post-operation period. The skull and the fleshed human head had a long sanctity in the Celtic world down many thousands of years. There is much evidence for this important cult in later Celtic religion and folklore. It is noteworthy that the roundel of bone removed in the operation of trepanning was regarded as apotropaic and magical, examples with holes bored through it near the edge, clearly for the purpose of suspension, having been found in graves.

The Celts would seem to have had a quite remarkable feeling for medicine and a very comprehensive knowledge and understanding of healing and apotropaic plants. There are wonderful passages in the rich repertoire of early Irish MSS, some of which describe in detail the various herbs which were used to heal those wounded in battle. Skilled physicians with a knowledge of surgery were also popular characters. Here we are commenting on the wider Celtic world but it is necessary to narrow our outlook in order to concentrate on what pertained to Wales. One can make a distinction between the dual rôle of the Welsh physician/surgeon and contrast this with the tradition in England of separate professions of physician and (barber-) surgeon. The fascination for the Welsh of everything pertaining to medicine and anatomy is clearly attested throughout the tradition. One interesting passage on the 'constituents of man' is alleged to have been the work of the sixth-century *pencerdd* (chief poet) Taliesin. The passage is entitled 'The Elements of Man':

> Man consists of eight parts: — the first is the earth, which is sluggish and heavy, whence is the flesh. The second is the stones, which are hard, and these are the materials of the bones. The third is water, which is moist and cold, and is the substance of the blood. The fourth is salt, which is briny and sharp, whence are the passions and the faculties of feeling, in respect of corporeal sense and perception. The fifth is the air, or wind, whence is the breath. The sixth is the sun, which is clear and fair, whence is the fire, or corporeal warmth, and the light and colour. The seventh is the Holy Spirit, whence are the soul and life. The eighth is Christ, that is the intellect and wisdom, and the light of the soul and life.
>
> If the part of man that preponderates be of the earth, he will prove unwise, sluggish and very heavy, and will be a little, short, thin dwarf, according as the preponderance may be, whether great or small. If it be of the air, the man will be light, unsteady, garrulous, and given to gossip. If of the stones, he will be hard of heart, understanding and judgement — a miser and a thief. If of the sun, he will be a man of genius, affectionate, active, docile, and poetical. If of the holy spirit, he will be godly, amiable, and compassionate, of a just and tender judgement and fond of the arts and sciences: and this cannot otherwise than equiponderate with Christ and divine sonship.

There are a few medical Triads allegedly dating to this period with the composition of which Taliesin is likewise accredited:

> There are three intractable substantial organs: the liver, the kidney and the heart.
> There are three intractable membranes: the dura mater, the peritoneum and the urinary bladder.
> There are three tedious complaints: disease of the knee joint, disease of the substance of a rib, and phthysis; for when purulent matter has formed in one of these, it is not known when it will get well.

The decades between the sixth and tenth centuries were fully taken up with troubles of a national kind, and the arts and sciences in Wales seem to have been neglected. This is indicated by the paucity of literary remains of that period, leaving us with no information about the state of the science of medicine nor about the status of the physician in the country in general. This is not however the case during the lifetime of that great compiler of the Welsh laws, Hywel Dda (the Good). His laws were promulgated somewhere in the middle of the tenth century, and those concerning the court physician were clearly set out, giving him and his art a clear and definable status.

The Mawddwy (Myddfai) Physicians

The Myddfai physicians consisted of a line of country doctors who lived in the parish of Myddfai, Carmarthenshire (*see* **40**). They have always aroused intense interest in Wales both because of the unusual feature of what one might call a 'practice' of family doctors as early as the thirteenth century. Their beginnings are associated with a story which survived in a series of medieval medical manuals. The oldest of these refers to a Rhiwallon Feddyg and his three sons, Cadwgan, Gruffudd and Einion who were doctors in the court of Rhys Gryg, Lord of Dinefwr in the thirteenth century. Myddfai was a manor in the territory of the lord Rhys and with the ending of the native Welsh princes was incorporated in the lordship of Llandovery. It is likely that a succession of these physicians continued in Myddfai right down to the eighteenth century. This succession of professional and well-educated families was typical of Celtic society and extended to and is paralleled by examples from Scotland (for example the Beatons of Dunvegan, Skye: *vide Companion to Gaelic Scotland*, p.22). In the last 200 years the skills of these physicians have attached themselves to a folk tale about Llyn y Fan Fâch.

The origin of the Meddygai Myddfai according to the legend of Llyn y Fan Fâch

In the twelfth century a widow lived near Llanddeusant in Carmarthenshire. Her husband had been a farmer but had fallen in the disastrous war of the Princes.

The widow was left with a son to rear, but good fortune came to her. In spite of her lonely state her livestock flourished and increased to such an extent that she was unable to find sufficient pasture for them on her own farm so she sent a proportion of them to the Black Mountain which adjoined her property. The cattle loved best the small lake on the north-western side of the hills known as the Carmarthenshire Vans. The lake was called *Llyn y Fan Fâch*, 'the Little Van Lake'. All went well and the boy grew to manhood and was customarily sent by his mother to take care of the cattle grazing on the mountain. One day, while he was walking along the edge of the lake, he was astounded to see, sitting on the surface of the water, a young woman. She was one of the most beautiful beings that had ever been seen by mortal eyes; her long hair fell over her shoulders in ringlets which she combed while using the calm surface of the lake as a mirror. Looking up, she saw the young man standing on the edge of the lake staring at her in astonishment and almost instinctively offering to her the barley bread and cheese which his mother had given him for his lunch when he left home. He was overcome by his feelings of love and admiration for this beautiful girl before him, and he continued to hold out his hand towards her, while she quietly drew nearer to him but would not accept the proffered food. He attempted to touch her but she avoided him, saying 'Your bread is hard-baked and I am not easy to catch', then she dived under the water and was gone from his sight, leaving the forlorn youth behind. He had no choice but to return home, bitterly disappointed and regretting that he had been unable to become better acquainted with the girl, whose beauty outshone that of all the girls he had ever seen. It is perhaps noteworthy that the parish of Myddfai used to be renowned for the beauty of its girls, but whether they were related to the lady of Lake Van or not is impossible to determine!

When he got home he told his mother about the astonishing vision he had witnessed. She told him to take some unbaked bread with him in his pocket, because there must have been some magic connected with the hard-baked bread that prevented him from taking hold of the girl. Next morning, before the sun had risen, the young man was at the lake, not only with the intention of looking after his mother's cattle but of trying to find the beautiful lake maiden he had seen the previous day. He looked everywhere and watched the surface of the lake, but only the ripples which were created by a fresh breeze stirred and a cloud hung ominously on the summit of the Van, all of which added to his misery and frustration.

Hours passed and then the wind dropped and the clouds which hid the Van Mountain from view dispersed before the strong light of the sun. Suddenly the youth was shocked to see that some of his mother's cattle had wandered almost to the opposite side of the lake, which was a precipitous and treacherous height. He remembered his duty and it compelled him to attempt to rescue them. He began to make haste to their aid when to his great joy the one he sought appeared before him as on the previous occasion and seemed to be even more divinely beautiful. He once again held out his hand to her, full of raw dough which he offered to her with his heart, vowing to love her forever. She refused everything, saying: 'Your bread is not baked; I will not have you', but as she vanished beneath the waters she smiled playfully at him and this aroused hopes in his heart which kept him from despair. As he made his way home he thought about her and was greatly cheered. His mother knew very well that he had not succeeded in his quest and she suggested that next time the bread he took should only be slightly cooked, as this was probably more pleasing to the mysterious girl with whom he had obviously fallen wildly in love.

Some instinct drove him early the following morning to leave home and to cross the mountain speedily. He soon reached the edge of the lake and impatiently waited for her to reappear and reassure him. The poor sheep and goats were browsing on the precipitous sides of the Van; the cattle were straying amongst the rocks and large stones; it rained and the sun shone from time to time, but the youth took no notice of them. All he was concerned about was the reappearance of the girl. He had been there through the morning and the afternoon, which now was fast turning into evening and night was not far off, but there was no sign of his beloved. The boy looked sadly over the waters and, to his amazement, saw some cows walking along its surface. Would they, he wondered, be followed by their mysterious mistress?

He was not disappointed, for the girl did reappear and to his lovesick eyes she was even more beautiful than before. She came towards the land and he rushed to meet her in the water. Her smile emboldened him to take her hand, nor did she refuse the lightly-baked bread which he offered to her. Moreover she consented to become his wife on condition that they should live together until he should strike her three times without a cause, and this is known as 'the three causeless blows' (*tri ergyd di-achos*). To such conditions he readily agreed; indeed he would have agreed to anything at the time. All he wanted was to secure her hand in marriage. And so the lady of the lake became engaged to the widow's handsome son and, letting go of his hand, she disappeared below the water. He was desperate with grief and almost decided to throw himself into the deepest water and to end his life.

He was on the very point of taking his own life, when out of the lake came two exquisite girls who were accompanied by an elderly, grey-haired man with a noble countenance and a firm, straight body, and with all the force and power of a young man. He spoke to the despairing youth in a soothing, gentle way, saying that as he, the widow's son, proposed to marry one of his daughters, he would agree to the marriage provided the youth was able to recognise which of the two girls before him was his beloved. This was no easy task because the girls were absolutely identical. It seemed to him a total impossibility to choose the right one and, should he take the wrong one, then all would be lost for all time. While he anxiously examined the two girls he was unable to perceive a single difference between them. Suddenly, one of them put her foot very slightly forwards. This movement, slight though it was, was observed by the youth, and he noticed some variation in the way in which they had tied their sandals. This small discovery instantly resolved the dilemma, for he had noticed on previous occasions the beauty of the lake girl's feet and ankles and the peculiarity of the way in which she tied her sandals. He boldly seized her hand. 'You have chosen aright', said her father, 'Be a good and faithful husband to her, and I will give her as a dowry as many cattle, horses, sheep and goats as she can count without drawing in her breath. But you must remember, if you are unkind to her at any time, and strike her three times without a cause, she and all her animals will return to me.'

So that was the marriage settlement to which the widow's son happily agreed, and his bride was asked to count the number of sheep she was to have. She immediately adopted an old mode of counting, by fives — one, two, three, four, five; one, two, three, four, five — and so on until the rapidity of her breath failed her and she was exhausted. The same process of counting was used to find out the number of goats, cattle and horses she would acquire and the full number of each species emerged from the lake the instant they were called by her father. Then the young couple were married, though we do not know anything about the ceremony, and afterwards went to live at a farm, Esgair Llaethdy, somewhat more than a mile from the village of Myddfai; they lived together in joy and prosperity for many years, and had three beautiful boys.

It came about that at one time a christening was to take place nearby, to which the young couple were invited. On the day, his wife seemed very unwilling to go to the christening, saying that the walk was too long for her. He told her to go and get one of the horses which were grazing nearby. She replied that she would, if he would get her gloves for her, which she had left behind in the house. He went to the house and came back with the gloves, and finding that she had not gone for the horse after all he playfully smacked her shoulder with one of the gloves, saying, 'Go, go.' She then reminded him of the terms of their marriage. He was not to strike her without a cause and had done so. She warned him to be more careful in future.

Another time they were together at a wedding. Guests had come from all the surrounding countryside and, with one thing and another, were full of high spirits and happiness. She, however, suddenly and with no apparent reason, burst into tears and sobbed alarmingly. Her husband touched her on her shoulder and asked the cause of her weeping. She told him: 'You are heading for trouble because that is the second time you have hit me without a cause.'

Years passed by. The children had grown up and they were remarkably brilliant young men. In the midst of so much happiness in his home the husband had almost forgotten that he could lose all the reasons for his happiness in a split second, were he to give her the third causeless blow. He was very careful in case any small happening should take place, which his wife would regard as a breach of their marriage contract. She had told him that as her love for him was as strong as ever, he must be careful lest through some careless act he should give her the third and last blow over which she herself had no control and which 'would separate them for ever'. It was her destiny. It came about that they were at a funeral and in the midst of the mourning and weeping and general grief she seemed to be in the highest spirits he had ever witnessed. She started to break into fits of uncontrollable laughter and this so deeply shocked her husband that he touched her, saying: 'Don't laugh!' She told him that she laughed because people when they die, are free from trouble, and getting up, she went out of the house saying, 'the final blow has been struck. Our marriage contract is cancelled and finished. Farewell.' Then she made off in the direction of Esgair Llaethdy and there called her cattle and other animals together, each by its own name. They all came to her at once. Her little black calf had been slaughtered, but it came alive again, and walked off with the rest of the stock at the command of their mistress. It was springtime and four oxen were ploughing in one of the fields. She called to them, and they came to her. And away they all went, animals and the lake lady, over the Myddfai mountain and to the lake from which they had come. Once there, all disappeared underneath the waters, only leaving behind a deep furrow made by the plough which the oxen pulled into the lake after them, which is there to this day to testify to the truth of the story.

The poor boys, her sons, often went down to the lake, hoping that their mother would come to them once more, but they were aware of her supernatural nature. On one of their walks, at a place near Dôl Howel at the Mountain Gate, still called *Llidiad y Meddygon*, the Physicians' Gate, she suddenly appeared, and addressed her eldest son, Rhiwallon, telling him that his calling was to benefit mankind by freeing them from pain and distress by healing every kind of disease. To help him achieve this, she gave him a bag full of medical prescriptions and instructions. She told him that if he paid strict attention to them, he and his family would become, for many generations thereafter, the most skilled physicians in the country. So promising to meet him when her advice was most badly needed, she disappeared. But on several occasions she met her sons on the banks of the lake and once she even went with them on their return home, as far as a place, the name of which still survives, *Pant y Meddygon*, the Dell of the Physicians. Here she showed them the various herbs and plants which grew there and informed them of their medical properties or virtues, and the knowledge she gave to them, together with their unrivalled brilliance, soon caused them to achieve a celebrity that no one before them had ever possessed. And so that their knowledge should never be lost, they wisely committed everything to writing for the good of mankind through all ages.

The story of the physicians of Myddfai has been handed down through many generations. Rhiwallon and his sons became physicians to Rhys Gryg, Lord of Llandovery and Dinefwr Castles, who awarded them with rank, lands and privileges at Myddfai so that they could continue in the practice of their art and science for the healing and benefit of all who should come to them for help. In this way they gave freely to those who could not afford payment the best medical advice and treatment. So the fame of the physicians of Myddfai spread over the whole country, and continued for many centuries among their descendants.

We have large numbers of the recipes used by these famous physicians for healing. Herbs and plants naturally are the main ingredients and these would seem to have been known down the long ages, handed down orally until they were committed to writing as recipes by the famed physicians of Myddfai. They are far too numerous for many to be included in this book, but I think it would be of interest to the reader to have some idea of the kind of recipes and remedies that were available.

> Toothache, that common evil that causes so much distress to the patient can be treated in the following way: 'Take distilled water of red roses, a small portion of beeswax, and a little fresh butter, say an equal quantity of each; let the ingredients be mixed together in a dish upon embers, then let a linen cloth be dipped herein and apply to the affected jaw as hot as it can be borne.' (*The Physicians of Myddfai*, John Pughe p.302)
>
> To heal a wound: 'Take yellow wax, melt on a slow fire, and take bruised cumin seed, mix with the molten wax, then stir these ingredients with a stirrer until cold. Apply this as a plaster to the wound.' (*op. cit.* p.303)
>
> For inflammation of the mammae: 'Take agrimony, betony, and vervain and pound well, then mix them with strong old ale, strain well and set some milk on the fire; when this boils add the liquor thereto and make a posset thereof, giving it to the woman to drink warm. Let her do this frequently and she will be cured.' (*op. cit.* p.310)
>
> For the bite of a mad dog: 'Seek some plantain, and a handful of sheep's sorrel, then pound well in a mortar with the whites of eggs, honey, and old lard, make it into an ointment and apply to the bitten part, so that it may be cured.' (*op. cit.* p.311)
>
> For a pain in the cardiac region: 'Take the centaury, pound well, boil in old ale and express well, afterwards boil to the half, take that with twice as much honey, and boil moderately; take a cup-ful thereof fasting for nine days, and it will remove the pain and oppression from the region of the heart without fail.' (*op. cit.* p.323)
>
> For a headache: 'Whoever is frequently afflicted with a headache let him make a lotion of the vervain, betony, chamomile, and a red fennel; let him wash his head three times a week therewith, and he will be cured.' (*op. cit.* p.333)

For pain or swelling in the thighs: 'Take a quart of sage wine and a handful of thyme, boil together, and when half boiled add some fresh butter, then boil down from a quart to a pint; when you go to bed wash your feet well therewith; then dip a linen cloth therein, and apply three or four fold to the painful members as hot as you can bear it for six or seven nights, it will do much good without doubt. If you have any brandy or blessed distillation, add a spoonful thereto when sufficiently boiled, mixing it well.' (*op. cit.* p.364)

For paralysis: 'Take a portion of rue, of coarse salt, of the white and yolk of an egg, and a little black soap [*I think this must be coal tar soap — Author*]; let the rue and salt be bruised together in a mortar, the egg and black soap being added thereto, mixing the whole well together. Apply it as a plaster to the affected part, and it will be cured.' (*op. cit.* p.387)

A sleeping potion: 'Take the juice of opium (poppy) (*see* **9**) and of eryngo, or of the seed of the latter, compound them into pills with milk, let these be ministered to the patient. One will induce sleep in general, but if not let him take another, and another again, if required, taking care that two or three hours should intervene between each dose in order to watch their effect before another is given.' (*op. cit.* p.400)

The following charm was administered by one the three sons of the lady of Lake Van:

A charm for uterine disease which was given by Rhiwallon the physician to Gwyrvyl, the daughter of Gruffydd ap Tewdwr — I adjure thee, thou diseased uterus by the Father, the Son, and the Holy Ghost, so that thou mightest not inflict pain, nor have power (for evil) in me, Gwyrvyl, the daughter of Rhys, the servant of God, either in the head, breast, stomach, or any other part of my body. Let God the Father prevail, let God the Son prevail, let God the Holy Ghost prevail. Even so be it. Amen.' (*op. cit.* p.454)

For the toothache: 'Get an iron nail and engrave the following words thereon: agla, Sabaoth, athanatos, and insert the nail under the affected tooth, then drive it into an oak tree, and whilst it remains there, the toothache will not return. But you should carve on the tree with the nail the name of the man affected with

> toothache, repeating the following: By the power of the Father, and these consecrated words, as thou enterest into this wood, so let the pain and disease depart from the tooth of the sufferer. Even so be it. Amen.' (*op. cit.* p.454)

The above are just an example of a large number of recipes for healing given by the physicians of Mawddwy. At the very end they have an interesting note of *Useful Things*. The list begins:

> Infusion. Pouring water or other fluid in a boiling state upon herbs or whatever other ingredient may be required.
> Decoction. Boiling the herbs or ingredients in the water or fluid required.
> Pottage or Porridge. Pouring boiling or cold water or other fluid such as may be required upon the herbs or other ingredients, leaving them to stand, then straining under a press.
> Soakage. Pouring cold or boiling water or other fluid on any substance capable of being influenced thereby, so as to become incorporated with what is poured thereupon.
> Confection. Fluids mixed with powders or other substances capable of being administered as a draught.
> Potion. A draught or fluid prepared according to art.
> Essence. An amorphous or odoriferous substance, which may be taken in a draught by mouth, or injected into the nostrils, head, rectum or other part.
> Electuary. Substances incorporated into a dough so as to be eaten.
> Constitution. The disposition which is in a man, or other living being, or herb, or other matter; being their virtue, inherent property, or nature.
> Pills. Incorporated medical substances, formed into small balls, so as to be taken at a gulp.
> Bath. An infusion or decoction in which the patient or his limb is to be put.
> Fomentation. To be applied as a wash to a hurt, whether hot or cold, as may be wanted.
> Regimen. The food and drink as regulated by medical advice.

Having looked at the list of *Useful Things* in detail, I think the next guide to medical treatment, entitled *The Essentials of a Physician*, should be left to the reader to peruse as they are lengthy, very detailed, and extremely interesting. Sufficient to say, the text begins with the words:

> These things should be in the possession of a physician: And then follow the characteristics which should distinguish him, which are called the Essentials of a Physician.

The first essential will be sufficient to indicate to the reader the nature of the essentials:

> A lancet to bleed or open an abscess, also a knife, somewhat larger.

The termination of this fascinating book on the Physicians of Myddfai ends with such interesting comments that I feel I should quote them in full here as they form a direct link with the Llyn y Fan Fâch story with which we began:

> And thus ends this Book of Medicine, and I, Howel the Physician, the son of Rhys, the son of Llewelyn, the son of Philip the Physician, have selected the same from the authorised Old Books of the original Physicians of Myddfai, even Rhiwallon the Physician, and his three sons Cadwgan, Gruffudd, and Einion, and the other Physicians, their sons and descendants, who succeeded them.
> And I, Howel the Physician, am regularly descended in the male line from the said Einion, the son of Rhiwallon the Physician of Myddfai, being resident in Cilgwryd, in Gower. May the grace and blessing of God attend this book, and him who studies it as a directory of the art, for the love of God, and the health of the diseased and maimed.
> Amen. With God's help even so let it be.

Morfydd E. Owen has contributed a perspicacious paper, *Medics and Medicine*, which deals largely with the court physicians and emphasises the universal Celtic tendency of cherishing and preserving whatsoever was archaic and traditionally founded in Celtic society.

Charms (*Swynion*)

The following entry in E. Owen (p.262) is entitled 'The Conjuror's Dress'. The word *conjuror* has somewhat misleading connotations. One imagines a stage on which one talented in conjuror's arts, for example pulling a white rabbit out of a hat or sawing in half a beautiful girl lying in a coffin-like box, and to find the word here causes some confusion until one remembers that conjuror has meanings other than that of the traditional stage magician. Personally, I believe that the so-called *conjuror* of whom Owen is writing in the following passage is closer to the old Druidic order of Vates or seers. The passage runs as follows, and this should help to clarify the case:

> Conjurors, when engaged in their *uncanny* [my emphasis] work, usually wore a grotesque dress, and stood within a circle of protection. I find so graphic a description of a doctor who dealt in divination in Mr Hancock's *History of Llanrhaiadr-yn-Mochnant*, Montgomery Collections Volume VI pp.329-30 that I will describe it:— 'He [the raiser of the devils] was much resorted to by the friends of parties mentally deranged, many of whom he cured. Whenever he assumed to practice the black art, he put on a most grotesque dress, a cap of sheepskin with a high crown, bearing a plume of pigeon's feathers, and a coat of unusual pattern, with broad hems, and covered with talismanic characters. In his hand he had a whip, the thong of which was made of the skin of an eel and the handle of bone. With this he drew a circle around him, outside of which, at a proper distance, he kept those persons who came to him, whilst he went through his mystic sentences and performances.'(Cf. the Irish Mogh Ruith, Ross, *Druids*)

Charms in general

Some believe that the curing of diseases by charms is purely due to superstition, and has nothing to do with common sense. In other words, it goes against orthodox medical practice and has no scientific grounds for success. However, the remarkable powers of the mind over material situations can hardly be doubted, hence the numerous miracle cures with which we are all familiar. If we can, as doctors believe, make ourselves ill due to negative thinking and attitudes, it is surely logical that the converse is the case and we all know the strength of the power of auto-suggestion. I think we can say without doubt that the so-called conjuror with his fancy dress and all its elaborate details was perhaps a folk remnant of the ancient tradition of the power of the pan-Celtic Vates: seers, prophets and healers. There are indeed, as Owen observes, 'undoubted cases of complete cures through the instrumentality of charms'.

Warts are one form of distressing affliction and they can, without doubt, be removed by faith in the power of the charmer to heal, and in his charms. Owen experienced many cases where the power of wart charms had the desired effect. Some of the simple cures which apparently have beneficial results which he lists (p.268) are, for example: the rubbing of the warts with the inside of a bean pod, which should then be thrown away; the rubbing of the warts with elderberry leaves plucked by night and then burnt, resulting in the disappearance of the warts; taking a piece of lean meat, wrapping this in paper, then throwing it behind one's own back and walking away without glancing backwards. The person who picks up the object will also pick up the warts! This seems rather an un-Christian sort of cure!

Styes (Llefrithen)

This painful condition was believed to be curable by taking a knitting needle and passing it backwards and forwards over the stye, but without touching it, at the same time counting its age in this way — one stye, two styes, up to nine and then counting backwards until you come down to one stye and no stye, this counting to be done in one breath. Should the charmer take a breath, he would break the charm but he could try the cure again twice more. This would ensure the healing of the stye and its disappearance within 24 hours.

Cattle charms (Swynion buchod)

These were of course of great importance and value if they succeeded, as cattle in general are prone to no end of accidents resulting in injuries and diseases such as scour, birth problems, mastitis and gastric ailments. Most importantly of all, they must be protected from hostile supernatural forces and the *llygad mal* or *llygad drug* ('evil eye') which enabled witches most commonly to steal the milk from the cattle and to inflict various other ailments and disasters upon them. One contributor to the Montgomeryshire Collections told the Rev. Owen (p.269 f) that he had in his possession two cattle charms that were actually used in order to protect the livestock of two small farms. As we are looking back to the late nineteenth century here, these are particularly valuable and worth quoting in full:

> In the name of the father and of the Son and of the Holy Ghost. Amen . . . and in the name of Lord Jesus Christ my redeemer, that I will give relief to . . . creatures his cows, and his calves, and his horses, and his sheep, and his pigs, and all creatures that alive be in his possession, from all witchcraft and from all other assaults of Satan. Amen.

He also states that:

> At the bottom of the sheet, on the left, is the magical word, *Abracadabra* [a word used as a charm, first found in 1696], written in the usual triangular form; in the centre, a number of planetary

> symbols, and on the right, a circular figure filled in with lines and symbols, and beneath them, 'By Jah, Joh, Jab.' It was the custom to rub these charms over the cattle a number of times, while some incantation was being mumbled. The paper was then carefully folded up, and put in a safe place where the animals were kept, to guard against future visitations.

Sometimes the charm was worn by the cattle, as we see below. This charm has a particular relevance to the appalling illness that has appeared over wide areas of the British Isles at the present time — it might be worthwhile for the distressed farmers to test the alleged powers of these ancient healing charms.

> *Charm for the foot and mouth disease*
> The cattle on a certain farm in Llansilin parish suffered from foot and mouth disease and old Mr H. . . . consulted a conjuror, who gave him a written charm which he was directed to place on the horns of the cattle, and he was told that this would act both as a preventive and a cure. This farmer's cattle might be seen with the bit of paper, thus procured, tied to their horns. My informant does not wish to be named, nor does she desire the farmer's name to be given, but she vouches for the accuracy of the information, and for my own use, she gave me all particulars respecting the above. This took place only a few years ago, when the Foot and Mouth Disease first visited Wales [*c.*1850].

The following charm was given to the Rev. Owen by the Vicar of Bryneglwys, which was procured for Mr Jones, Tynywern, Bryneglwys, Denbighshire, who had it from his uncle by whom it was used at one time. Owen goes on to state that it was not easy to decipher the charm and four of the words towards the end are quite illegible therefore he has omitted them. The translation indicates the nature of the charm, which begins in the name of the Trinity. All charms in a Christian milieu, although they may be pagan in origin, tend to be fully integrated into Christianity, in which faith they have been accepted.

> In the Name of the Father, the Son, and
> the Spirit.
> May Christ Jesus the sanctified one, who
> suffered death on the cross,
> When thou didst raise Lazarus from his
> tomb after his death,
> When thou forgavest sins to Mary
> Magdalene, have mercy on me, so that

everything named by me and
crossed by me + may be saved by the
power and virtue
of thy blessed words my Lord Jesus
Christ. Amen.

Jesus Christ our Lord save us from every
kind of temptation whether spiritual
above the earth
or under the earth, from the devilish
man or woman
with evil heart who bewitcheth the goods
of their owner;
his evil virtue, his evil excommunicated
heart
cut off from the Catholic Faith + by
the power and virtue
of thy blessed words my Lord Jesus
Christ. Amen.
Jesus Christ our Lord save us from the
disease and the
affliction, and the wrath and the envy,
and the mischief, and
the . . . and the planet of the sky and the earthly
poison, by the power and virtue
of thy Blessed words, my Lord Jesus Christ. Amen.

The +s indicate that crosses were here made by the person who used the charm, and probably the words of the charm were audibly uttered.

Another cattle charm spell

Mr Hughes, Plasnewydd, Llansilin, lost several head of cattle. He was told to bleed one of the herd, boil the blood, and take it to the cow-house at midnight. He did this, and lost no more cows after applying this charm.

A charm for calves

If calves were scoured [had diarrhoea; 1764] too frequently and it was in danger of killing them, a hazel twig the length of the calf was twisted round the neck like a collar, and it was supposed to cure them.

As these charms are old, very precious and becoming extremely difficult to collect in the field, I feel it is worthwhile quoting the last one as well in full (p.273). It is entitled *Charms Performed with Snake's Skin*:

1 Burn the skin and preserve the ashes. A little salve made out of the ashes will heal a wound.
2 A little of the ashes placed between the shoulders will make a man invulnerable.
3 Whoso places a little of the ashes in water with which he washes himself, should his enemies meet him, they will flee because of the beauty of his face.
4 Cast a little of the ashes into thy neighbour's house and he will leave it.
5 Place the ashes under the sole of thy foot, and everybody will agree with you.
6 Should a man wrestle, let him place some of the ashes under his tongue, and no-one can conquer him.
7 Should a man wish to know what is about to occur to him, let him place a pinch of the ashes on his head, and then go to sleep, and his dreams will reveal the future.
8 Should a person wish to ascertain the mind of another, let him throw a little of the ashes on that person's clothes, and then let him ask what he likes, the answer will be true.
9 Whosoever wishes to make his servant faithful, let him place the ashes in the clothes of his servant, and as long as they remain there he will be faithful.
10 If a person is afraid of being poisoned in his food, let him place the ashes on the table with his food, and poison cannot stay there with the ashes.
11 If a person wishes to succeed in love, let him wash his hands and keep some of the ashes in them, and then everybody will love him.
12 The skin of the adder is a remedy against fevers.

Charms for shingles

The custom of charming for shingles (*ryri*) was, according to T.W. Hancock's *The History of Llanrhaiadr-yn-Mochnant*, more frequently performed in this parish than in any other in Montgomeryshire. Both the charmer and the patient were to fast before meeting in the morning of the healing process. It was a simple method of cure. The healer simply breathed gently over that area of the sufferer's body which was inflamed. The healer then gently spat on the inflammation and around it. A few visits to the charmer were seemingly sufficient to bring about a cure; sometimes the charmer's powers of healing were so great that one visit would suffice. The power of healing the shingles in this manner was alleged to have disappeared altogether; it would not appear to have been practised in this parish for many years. The possession of this remarkable healing power by the charmer who had to fast so rigorously beforehand was believed to have been derived from the charmer's having eaten eagle's flesh, or it having been eaten by an ancestor up to the ninth generation back. The belief was that the virtue was transmitted from the person who had eaten the flesh to his descendants for nine generations. The reason for this dislike of the eagle was believed to have originated by the shingles having been introduced into the area by a hostile eagle. The charm went as follows:

> *Yr Eryr Eryres*
> Mi a'th ddanfonais
> Dros naw m'r a thros naw mynydd
> A thros naw erw o dir anghelfydd
> Lle na chyfartho ci, ac na frefo fuwch
> Ac na ddelo yr eryr Byth yn uwch
>
> Male eagle, female eagle
> I send you
> Over nine seas, and over nine mountains
> And over nine acres of unprofitable land
> Where no dog shall bark, and no cow shall low,
> And where no eagle shall higher rise.' (p.264 *ibid.*)

Charm for clefyd y galon, *heart disease*

The Rev. J. Felix, vicar of Cilcen, near Mold, when a young man, lodged in Eglwysfach, near Conwy. His landlady, noticing that he looked pale and thin, suggested that he was suffering from *clefyd y galon*, which may be translated as above, or as lovesickness, a complaint common enough in young people, and she suggested that he should call in David Jenkins, a respectable farmer and a local preacher with the Wesleyans, to cure him. Jenkins came, and asked the supposed sufferer whether he believed in charms. He proceeded with his patient as if he had answered in the affirmative. Mr Felix was told to take his coat off, and he did so, and then he was bidden to tuck up his shirt above his elbow. Mr Jenkins then took a yarn thread and, placing one end on the elbow, measured to the tip of Felix's middle finger. Then he told his patient to take hold of the yarn at one end, and the other end resting the while on the elbow, and he was to take fast hold of it, and stretch it. This he did and the yarn lengthened and this was a sign that he was actually sick of heart disease. Then the charmer tied this yarn around the patient's left arm above the elbow, and there it was left, and on the next visit measured again, and he was pronounced cured. 'The above information I received from Mr Felix, who is still alive and well.' He concludes:

> Sufficient has been said about charms to show how prevalent the faith in their efficacy was. Ailments of all descriptions had their accompanying antidotes; but it is singularly strange that people professing the Christian religion, should cling so tenaciously to its forms, so that even in our own days [late nineteenth century] such absurdities as charms find a resting-place in the minds of our rustic population, and often, even the better-educated classes resort to charms for obtaining cures for themselves and their animals.

But from ancient times, omens, charms, and auguries have held considerable sway over the destinies of men.

Divination

One method of divination was known in west and mid-Wales as the Bible and Key Divination, which would enable one to find out the first two letters of the name of one's future wife or husband was, according to Caredig Davies, very common, even in the early twentieth century. It was practised by young members of both sexes. The usual procedure was as follows. A small bible was lifted and once it was opened the key of the front door was placed on the sixteenth verse of the first chapter of Ruth:

> And Ruth said, entreat me not to leave thee, or to return from following after thee; for whither thou goest, I will go; and where thou lodgest, I will lodge; my people shall be thy people, and thy God my God.

Some people put the key in chapter VIII of Solomon's Song, verses 6 and 7, instead of on the book of Ruth. Then the bible was closed and tied round with the garter taken off the left leg of the girl or young man who wished to know his or her future wife or husband's initials. It was considered impossible for one person to perform this ceremony alone; he must enlist the help of a friend. The young suitor had to put the middle finger of his right hand under the loop of the key and take care that the bible remained steady. Then the one who was not consulting the future repeated the above verse or verses, and when he came to the appointed letter, that must be the first letter of his future wife's name, the bible would turn round under the finger. Davies heard at Ystradmeurig that a few years ago:

> a young woman, a farmer's daughter, tried this bible and key divination; and whilst the ceremony was going on, and her sister

> assisting her to hold the key under the bible and repeating the words, instead of the book turning around as she expected, she saw a coffin moving along the room, which was a sign that she was doomed to die single, and so it came to pass!

The farmhouse in which the above young woman lived still stands and is sited near Ystrad Fflur (Strata Florida), Cardiganshire; Davies however was reluctant to name the house. He said that he had personally witnessed this divination being carried out once or twice but that he never once heard of the coffin appearing, apart from the case just mentioned (p.13-14).

Divination by the teacup

Divination by the position of tealeaves when a teacup has been drained of its liquid is a very widespread practice and was certainly regularly carried out on both sides of my own family. In Wales, it was commonplace for young girls — who were always anxious to know what the future held for them in respect of love and marriages, the appearance of future husbands (or non-appearance, as the case may be) — to take part. This was especially popular with young people who were in love with each other and intended to marry. There was a particular woman in the parish of Llandysul who was an expert at reading cups. She lived in a small village, Pont Shaen, in Cardiganshire, and many young women and young men went to her for augury. There was another cup-reader living near Llandovery in Carmarthenshire *c.*1911, to whom young girls went for consultation.

Welsh women were exceptionally fond of tea and they were quite able to read omens by means of the tealeaves without having to go to others who were supposed to be experts in the art. When several of them met together for tea, they assisted one another in reading their cups, for tea-drinking was the order of the day amongst the women of Wales. Once the cup was drained, it was turned round three times in the left hand, bottom up, and left to drain for a few minutes before being closely examined. Should the tealeaves be scattered evenly round the sides of the cup, leaving the bottom perfectly clear, it was regarded as a very good omen; on the other hand, when the bottom of the cup was black with tealeaves, it was a very bad omen. Some trouble and misfortune would be imminent.

When the leaves made a ring on the side of the cup, it meant that the girl who consulted the cup would marry very soon. On the contrary, if the ring was at the bottom of the cup she would have disappointment in love and could even be doomed to die single. When the tealeaves formed into a cross or even a coffin, that was naturally considered to be a bad omen, but as a rule, a horse, dog or bird portended well. Two leaves seen in close proximity to the side of the cup foretold a letter bringing good news. Again, when there was a speck floating on the surface of the cup of tea before drinking, some people believed it meant a letter, a parcel or a visitor was coming. If the young girl should take it to represent her lover, she would prove his fidelity by placing the speck on the back of her left hand and striking it with the back of her right hand. Should the speck or the small tealeaf leave the back of the left hand and cling and stick fast to the right hand when striking it, this would indicate that the young man was faithful. But if it should happen that the tealeaf still remained on the left hand where it was placed, especially after striking it three times, the young man was not to be depended upon. Some women could even tell by means of the teacup what trade their admirer followed, the colour of their future husband's hair, and many other such details.

The Grail

Celtic medieval literature was much concerned with the ritual of feasting in the houses of the noble leaders and their retinues. Feasts require vessels, and, as magic plays a large rôle in the medieval Welsh (and Irish) tales, there were various dishes from bowls to plates and platters, often of rich metals and jewelled adornments, which had the ability never to be empty, no matter how large the gathering or how hungry the guests. There was also one other such vessel possessing magical qualities of largesse and this fascinated the medieval writers. One of the major themes in medieval Welsh literature is the search by eminent knights for this vessel. We know it as the Holy Grail — in medieval French *la sainte Graal* — and many legends are focused on this mysterious dish. Although it is associated with Christianity the motif of the never-empty vessel belongs to a much more archaic milieu.

For the present it is sufficient to concentrate upon the origin of the Christian legend of the Holy Grail. Joseph of Arimathea is believed to have taken the vessel used by Christ, a cup of some kind, while distributing food and drink to his disciples at the Last Supper. When Christ was crucified, Joseph was at the foot of the cross with the cup in which he collected some blood from the sacred sacrifice. Details are difficult to come by but it would seem that Joseph was a trader and it is even believed in some quarters that on one of his journeys to Britain he was accompanied by the boy Christ. This supposition is echoed in William Blake's beautiful hymn 'And did those feet, in ancient time, walk upon England's mountains green? And was the Holy Lamb of God on England's pleasant pastures seen?' If this is to be believed, then Joseph brought the Holy Grail, the sacred vessel, to Glastonbury after the crucifixion, as well as a cutting from the thorn tree from which Christ's cruel crown was fashioned.

Between this period in the first century AD and the Grail legends in medieval European tradition, long centuries elapsed and the Grail mysteriously disappeared. The search for it (the quest for the Holy Grail) was undertaken by many brave knights including Celtic warrior heroes. Some of the best medieval literature is that contained in Welsh manuscripts. The fascination of the Grail has never waned and even today its mystery has not been resolved. Many vessels throughout the country claim to be the original Grail and one in particular, the Nanteos cup (see below), was accredited with having been the True Grail, possessing magical powers of healing.

The Nanteos cup

There is a beautiful eighteenth-century mansion at Nanteos, near Aberystwyth, which stands in superb wooded grounds and possesses a fine lake and many ancient and splendid trees. It has not had an altogether happy history, and there are several stories about hauntings which take place at intervals during the year. Belief in these is now weakening as modern conditions and the influence of television displace them. However, there is a strange atmosphere in the house and the well in particular has ghostly associations. It was the home of the Powells, a rich family, the sons of which were sadly killed during the war. Although the splendid house and its associated buildings are sufficient attraction in themselves, the fact that the Powells owned and still own the famous Nanteos cup (**41**) — renowned for its powers of healing the sick — has made it a place of considerable pilgrimage. The vessel has given rise to many stories as to its ultimate origin and powers. It was eventually moved for safekeeping to a bank in Hereford, where it is held in the vaults; it may, however, be returned to Nanteos for the purpose of healing in conjunction with the special qualities of the well.

The cup itself is known in Welsh as the *Ffiol* and people, not only of Welsh ancestry, come from all over the world to seek the healing virtues of the cup. The water, which forms a major part in the healing process has to come from the well, the virtues of which in conjunction with those of the cup make the healing possible. People have such faith in the powers of the cup that, if they are very ill or near death, they often request that a bottle of water filled from the cup should be sent to them with all due haste; many claim that they have benefited from this even when on the very verge of death. However, this cannot go on indefinitely. In Wales as in Gaelic Scotland it is believed that too frequent a use of a vessel or well will eventually weaken and finally destroy any powers of healing.

The story goes that the cup originally came from the Holy Land and is of great age. The wood is very dark. The Grail cup, having according to tradition been brought first of all to Glastonbury by Joseph of Arimathea from the Holy Land, was then traditionally taken to the abbey of Ystrad Fflur, near

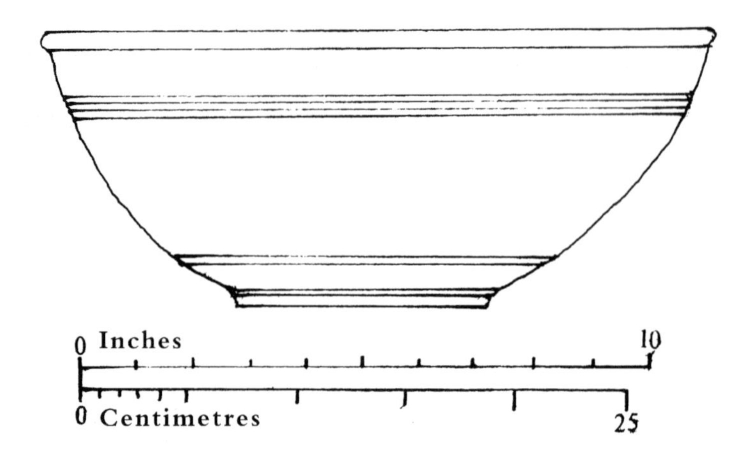

41 *Sketch of the 'Holy Grail', formerly at Nanteos, Cardiganshire (Ceredigion), based on a drawing of the remains of the 'Healing Cup' on p.294 of J.C. Davies* Folklore of West and Mid Wales, *Aberystwyth, 1911 and Lanerch, 1992*

Pontrhydfendigaid, Cardiganshire, and then to Nanteos, where it carried out many cures, being especially efficacious in the case of haemorrhage. Surprisingly, it has seemingly never been subjected to such scientific tests as radiocarbon dating. Many people claim to have found or acquired the original Grail, assuming such really exists, but the Nanteos cup would seem to have as good a claim as any.

10 Fairies, supernatural birds and animals

The origin of the fairies

Belief in fairies and fairy lore was not, like many other things, peculiar to the Celtic peoples, but is found widely throughout the world in various forms. At present, our particular interest must be focused on the concepts of this mysterious race, as it was envisaged throughout Wales. The usual name for this unearthly race is the *Tylwyth Teg*. They were also known as *Bendith y Mamau* (the mothers' blessing). Another supernatural tribe or people were known as *Ellyll* (elf or goblin). The fairies were regarded by most peoples as being on the whole dangerous to humanity and thus in need of constant propitiation. However, they could also be helpful to mankind if proper respect were given to them. They were notorious for stealing healthy babies who had been put out in the sunshine while the busy mother took the opportunity to get on with her chores. In the Scottish Highlands, and probably in Wales also, iron was a most powerful weapon against them and so the long iron tongs used for the peat or wood fires used to be taken outside and placed across the cradle of the sleeping infant. These would protect the little one from theft by the fairies. Until within living memory in many places, a bowl of milk or some food was put out last thing at night to please these supernatural beings and so protect the household from harm.

Many people claimed to have seen the fairies. I myself have never done so to my knowledge, but I have spoken to many people who have described these Otherworldly people. Contrary to general belief that they are small, dainty creatures, rather like great dragonflies, my informants have always spoken of them as being up to 3ft in height. Despite their ability to aid mankind, they were nearly always held in superstitious awe. It is a widespread motif that they lived in fairy mounds, which no man could enter freely but could be lured into, where time did not exist in human terms and from which it was very difficult to escape. Those who managed to do so were astonished to find they had returned to a completely changed world. Often, instead of having made merry with these strange beings for an hour or so, as they thought, they had been away for one or more centuries. Their families had been lying in the graveyard for many years, their dwellings were often in ruins and they recognised very little about the place which they believed they had left so recently. Often their own demise followed soon after their return and they virtually crumbled into dust, being now of a great age. Another belief concerning the fairies was that they were really the souls of the dead but I think there is little to support this theory.

There were, and still are, many stories about the *Tylwyth Teg*, and some families claim to be descended from a fairy woman who married a mortal. The motif of the marriage taking place only on condition that the husband would never strike his fairy wife is very widespread in the Celtic countries and Wales has recorded several good examples. These tend to be somewhat lengthy and complicated but the motif is of the fairy bride telling her suitor that she would only consent to a marriage with him on condition that he should never strike her, usually with iron. They marry and live together happily for many years and children are born to them. However, it is inevitable that such happiness must end. Always by chance, the husband succeeds, to his horror, in inadvertently striking his wife with an iron object which is intended for another purpose. For example, stirrups being put on a horse touch her leg and she immediately disappears, or a blow meant for the anvil, for example, accidentally strikes the girl, with the same sad result. In the story just recounted, it was the iron stirrups which resulted in the termination of the marriage. Three or four children had been born from the union and people believed — and may yet believe — they had met or had knowledge of their descendants.

The Welsh fairies, as we have seen, could be known by several different names, amongst them *Tylwyth Teg*, *Bendith y Mamau* and *Dynon Bach Teg* (little fair folk). This last was a Pembrokeshire name. In the non-Welsh-speaking region of Pembrokeshire, people who lose their way, especially at night, were said to be pisky-led. Pisky of course stands for pixie. Other groups of elf-like or fairy beings called *bwbach*, *bwca*, *bwci*, *bwgan*, *coblyn* and *ellyll* are sometimes classified as fairies. *Bwca* also appears as *pwca* (Puck?). *Bwbach* meant 'to scare' in the fourteenth century. The female fairies were very beautiful creatures and usually helpful, living communally. They were also generally benevolent. Sometimes they kept close to the fire, living, it is alleged, under the hearthstone at a farm near Aberdaron. Sometimes the fairy women fell in love with humans and took men for their husbands and bore them children. Apart from the coblin which makes a knocking sound in the mines the other sprites are ill-intentioned and malevolent.

The fairies live, as we have seen, in a community, which has as its king Gwyn ap Nudd. This is an interesting name and it is not unlikely that it is of Irish origin. Gwyn is the linguistic equivalent of Finn and Nudd is the Welsh equivalent of Irish Nuadu and the god Nodons or Nodens, the god who presided over his sanctuary at Lydney Park, Gloucestershire, overlooking the River Severn. It is a dramatically beautiful place, and in this general area much folklore about the old gods still lingers. Sul Minerva, equated with Sulis, was goddess of the healing waters of Aquae Sulis (Bath), waters which incidentally harboured a considerable number of metal curse-tablets. Sul was certainly a non-Roman goddess of great power, whose shrine may have been on the hill above the baths, known as Little Solbury. Excavations were started there recently, and may bring about interesting results.

In the life (*Buchedd*) of St Collen, which is more legendary and supernatural than hagiographical, Collen is at some time alleged to have become Abbot of Glastonbury and then retired in order to lead an extremely austere life on Glastonbury Tor. Glastonbury Tor was the legendary home of a certain tribe of fairies and Collen had a dangerous encounter on the Tor with Gwyn ap Nudd, King of Annwn, the Otherworld or Underworld, and of the fairies. This threatened to be a dangerous situation for the man of God but he kept his nerve, sprinkled Gwyn with holy water from a bottle which he habitually carried with him, and overcame him. He immediately left his retreat and proceeded to a sanctuary which may have been Llangollen, *Llan* being 'church' and *Collen* the name of the saint. He is said to have been venerated as a saint in Cornwall and Brittany.

The saint described in some small measure his experience when he glimpsed the interior of Glastonbury Tor in which the Otherworld was allegedly situated. It was full of fairies dancing and merry-making and distributing delicious-looking food with which they tempted Collen but which he staunchly refused to eat. It is generally known that if one finds oneself by some means or another inside a fairy dwelling-place, it is fatal to eat any morsel of fairy food, no matter how tempting it may be.

Fairies play an important rôle in all Celtic folklore and I have talked to many people in Celtic areas, Highland and Island, Scotland and Wales and Ireland, who claim to have seen these not-so-little people. The *Tylwyth Teg* are at the centre of many Welsh legends but space does not permit me to dwell on them in greater detail. Rhys quotes a strange tale from Conwy Vale from an informant of his who knew that fairies lived for seven years on the earth, seven years in the air, and seven years under the ground. There they were known as *plant Rhys ddwfn*, which means 'the children of Rhys of the Deep'. Jones questions this statement (p.53) as being doubtful unless it conceals some Goidelic influence, as is quite possible. There are strong Irish undertones here.

Supernatural birds and animals

There were widespread beliefs in Wales, as in the other Celtic countries, that the land was not only inhabited by ordinary animals — sheep, goats, pigs, dogs and others — but by numerous mythological creatures, often closely resembling the more familiar animals, but possessing powers baleful and benign which soon made it obvious to those who came into close contact with them that these were no earthly creatures. Many were believed to belong to the *Tylwyth Teg* or fairies. Some were owned by even more sinister figures, whose acquaintance we shall briefly make in the course of this chapter. The Otherworld dogs are known as *Cwn Annwn* and are sometimes described in English as Hell-dogs, or hounds of Hell. In Wales they may also be called *Cwn Wybir* ('sky dogs') and *Cwn Bendith y Mamau*. One description, given by Owen p.125 ff of his *Welsh Folklore*, of these fairy dogs is as follows: the 'Fairy Pigs' consisted of a pack of small hounds which were headed by a large dog. They made a blood-curdling baying which put the fear of death into all who heard it, which is not surprising for it portended death! In other words, they resembled Gaelic banshees. All normal dogs stopped barking and raced back to their kennels. The birds were silent in the groves as soon as they heard the fairy dogs' baying, and as they approached, the owl itself was silent. When the terrible howl of the Hell-hounds was heard all fell silent in the house. Young people ceased laughing and all the talk round the fireside came to an abrupt end. They must indeed have been intimidating creatures, as the human beings, upon hearing their terrible cries, grew pale and began to tremble with fear, huddling together protectively. The worst thing of all was the fact that these animals were actually foretelling the imminent death of someone in the immediate locality. Crossroads were particularly popular with these Hell-hounds, and they made an even more alarming bawling there. If anyone dared to interfere with them, they would bite and haul the unfortunate person away with them; their bite alone often proved fatal to the victim. They would gather in great numbers in the churchyard, in which the burial they had foreseen was to take place. Moreover, their infallible instinct indicated to them the spot where the grave would be dug, where they would sink into the earth and disappear.

This is a very alarming description of belief in the supernatural carried to an extreme but it is by no means unique to Wales. Usually in other Celtic traditions it is a single black dog that threatens the traveller and sometimes brings about his death. In my own, Scottish, family it is the fox that acts as the banshee. There was no record, however, of these sinister animals ever harming any other creature, human or animal, if they were not provoked. It was generally believed, however, that certain supernatural hounds could be heard on wild, stormy nights in close pursuit of the souls of unbaptised babies and those who had not received the rites and holy blessings before death. Belief in these dogs was widely and deeply held.

These dogs were usually described as being white with red ears. This takes us right back to Celtic mythology, being a close description of the Otherworld dogs one encounters in older documents. An old man described them, saying their colour was blood-red, they were always dripping with gore, and their eyes and teeth were like fire. He had never seen the dogs himself, but had heard tales of them. As Owen goes on to say, these are clearly the dogs that Pwyll, Prince of Dyfed encountered when he went hunting and carelessly set his own dogs on a stag which had been killed by a pack of magical dogs, brilliant white with red ears. Such Otherworld animals occur frequently in medieval tales of Wales. See, for example the story of Pwyll Pendeuic Dyvet (Pwyll Lord of Dyvet) in Williams, Ifor, Pedeir Keinc y Mabinogi, p.1ff.

The Otherworld cow

There are numerous tales from most, if not all the Celtic countries about a supernatural or fairy cow which behaved in various singular ways and which was able to supply an entire township with milk, provided it was properly treated. Any misuse of this nourishing substance would cause the milk to dry up and the animal would disappear and go to some other village or township. Stories about this magical creature are to be found widely in Wales, either in wild mountain country or in the lush valleys for which Wales is renowned. *Y Fuwch Frech* — 'The Speckled Cow' — was alleged to have had her home on the open mountain side.

Elias Owen managed to obtain a piece of interesting oral tradition concerning the magic animal directly from one Thomas Jones of Cefn Bannog in the same region, near Ruthin, Clwyd. The following is a précis of his interesting fieldwork in the area. He was told that long ago a marvellous cow was pastured on the hill close to the farm, Cefn Banawg, which took its name from the mountain ridge. She was well cared for and several place names attest to her popularity. A trackway led from the ruined cow-house to a spring named *Ffynnon y Fuwch Frech* (Spring of the Speckled Cow), from which the cow habitually drank. It used to graze on a pasture known as Waun Banawg, not far away. Remains of ruins in such regions show the walls to have been several feet thick, ideal for keeping out cold and wet in the dark winter months. It is an isolated place but the ancient house had a plenitude of heather and ferns. The local tradition was that this cow was the mother of the mythical horned *Ychain Banawg* (large oxen). The people of Denbighshire loved to tell stories about this speckled cow and recited a remarkable story about it which was handed down from generation to generation, an interesting indication of the strength of the oral tradition in Wales. People in need of milk used to carry a bucket to this cow, and no matter how large a vessel they took, there was always enough rich milk to fill the pail full. This ready supply of good milk continued for a long time and people went constantly to the cow, which gave generously of its largesse to one and all. But this was, like all good things, to come abruptly to an end through magical intervention. An evil hag was envious of the good fortune of the people and she took a sieve in her hand and went to attempt to milk the poor cow dry. She milked it and milked it into the sieve and in the end there was no more milk to be got. The cow took great offence at this treatment and instantly went away and no one ever saw her again.

However, there is a tradition that she made for a lake four miles away, with her two offspring, the Dau Eidion Banawg (the two long-horned oxen) to the lake known as *Llyn Dau Ychain* (the lake of the two oxen) near Cerrig-y-Drudion, and they all disappeared under the water and were seemingly never again seen. A similar tale is told in the Scottish Highlands (*vide* Ross, *Folklore of the Scottish Highlands* p.68ff). There is another version of the tale of the speckled cow concerning her two calves, the long-horned oxen. When they were fully-grown, they were renowned for their strength and they had a unique power of banishing evil spirits, one of which haunted the Church at Cerrig-y-drudion terrorising the local people. After a terrible struggle, the brave oxen managed to overcome the evil one by driving it into the waters of the lake where they themselves were drowned.

The crane

The crane has always held an intense fascination for the Celtic peoples onto whose lands it used to migrate, or which they would encounter on journeys to other countries. This is not in any way a cause of wonder, the bird being of a strange and elegant beauty, its appearance more fitting to the Otherworld than to more mundane surroundings. No longer a resident in the British Isles, this magnificent bird, with its long, slender legs by means of which it is able to run at great speed comparable to that of a horse, inevitably attracted a large body of folklore and superstitious belief. Its small but purposeful head, set on a long, slender neck, its huge drooping wings as it grazed in the grain-fields of Europe and the British Isles — to which it migrated in flocks composed of hundreds of birds — and its buoyant, expressive tail mark it out as one of the wonders of the avian world. Pure white in colour and combining a stunning beauty with so many practical abilities, it is little wonder that the pagan Celtic world and the early Christian peoples alike were deeply awed by this strange migratory creature. In early Ireland it was regarded as one of the forms adopted by a powerful goddess connected with warfare. After the coming of Christianity to the British Isles it would seem to have been held in some affectionate regard by the Church. See Ross, *Druids*, p.140ff for the story of St Columba and the crane.

In parts of Scotland it was especially closely associated with death and there were several expressions in which the crane was clearly regarded as the agent of death. There is one saying from the eastern Highlands of Scotland: 'Will he come or will he go, or will he eat the flesh of cranes?' It is clear from this that to eat the flesh of this bird was forbidden by tabu. It was believed to bring about the immediate end of one whose dying had taken too long. Another interesting means of bringing about the same result was to say: 'Cran's flesh or ran's flesh come out your way.' '*Cran*' means crane in Scots and '*ran*' is for raven. This indicates that it was unlucky to eat the flesh of either of these species. In Wales there were many bird superstitions in the folklore of the people. One of these which has been recorded by Elias Owen (p.321) is the belief held that a crane flying upstream is requesting wet weather. If she flies downstream, she seeks good weather. The same applied to the heron. Another strange belief was that, at the waning of the moon, the crane grew thin, and at its waxing she was fat.

*The peacock (*paun*)*

I had not expected to find any peacock lore in Wales, but I came across one legend which held that to hear the bird screeching at night was an omen of impending death. I thought nothing of this until that same night when I entered the bedroom and heard an unearthly noise like a cat in distress. I opened every drawer and cupboard and searched while the noise continued, but could find nothing. Then, on looking out of the window I saw, to my amazement and disquiet, a large and beautiful peacock strutting about our drive and several terrified cats crouching in long grass and up trees. It has never left us and the cats are now devoted to it. If one annoys it, it raises its great wings and tail showing its bright blue feathers and does an elegant dance in front of them. Now they all sit outside together in the sunshine and it is clear that Parry Peacock has come to stay. Where he fits into Welsh bird-lore I am not sure, but he is a colourful addition to our own large complement of wild birds of every kind — and he enjoys their food and then goes to sleep on the garden seat outside my study window.

Other bird beliefs

There were many bird beliefs in Wales. The soul of a dying person was alleged to take on bird form and fly from the mouth of the one whose end was close. A bird tapping on the window was sometimes regarded with superstitious awe, usually portending the death of some member of the family. An owl seen during the day boded ill and often portended death (nor have all these signs and omens entirely disappeared; people perhaps tend to speak less openly about them). This was known as *Aderyn corff*. When a person was seriously ill and brought to bed it was a widespread belief that the arrival of a bird fluttering its wings against the window of the room in which the afflicted person lay was a sure sign that death was soon to follow. Sometimes the bird not only beat its wings against the window but uttered a strange shrieking noise then and on its departure. The death bird was often believed to be the owl, tawny or screech, and its widespread association with death has made it a creature to be regarded with superstitious fear and often positive dislike. This feeling would of course be enhanced by the fact that the bird is very unpopular with the other birds which tend to attack it.

A crowing hen is supposed to portend death or bad news for a member of a family, or indeed of the entire family. The poor creature who had dared to crow like a cock and therefore displayed unnatural tendencies was immediately killed.

Owen also notes another custom (p.298) which has certainly never come my way in Scotland or indeed anywhere else. If a hen should lay a very small egg, it was to be taken and thrown backwards over the head and over the roof of the house to prevent a death occurring.

There was quite a lot of folklore current in Owen's time about the habits of rooks who, of course, live in colonies rather than singly, in nests. As we all know, the habits of birds change from time to time and birds will arrive and settle in an area or the grounds of private property apparently at random. Sometimes there is very good reason for this change occurring. For example, a new building is put up on places where birds used to nest; or an old barn or byre is nailed up or destroyed, and year after year the poor birds — martins and swallows, for example — will come back trying to find a place where they can build their nest, eventually giving up and finding some new terrain.

Owen has some interesting stories on this theme: the rook seems to be particularly attached to the colony, where many birds have their nests and lay their eggs there each year. He quoted his own experience while visiting the parkland of a gentleman's estate where a colony of rooks had apparently resided for generations. It was regarded as a bad omen that the birds suddenly departed carrying their nesting material with them. He was told that this was indeed a very bad omen and signified that ill luck would strike the excellent family who occupied the old premises. Owen went on to visit a friend who lived nearby in another gentry-house which was situated about two miles from the park which had been rejected by the birds. He commented on this phenomenon to the lady of the estate and she responded with a knowing smile. She told him that a strange thing had happened: a colony of rooks had quite taken over all the great trees that surrounded her house. He wished her luck, fully aware that this was where the rooks had settled. Both of the above stories relate to East Denbighshire.

Owen also himself remembers an occasion when a rookery was deserted by the birds shortly before ill-fortune descended upon those who occupied the house round which the trees were growing. The owner observed one morning that his rooks were carrying away their nests to some new home. He asked his servant to follow the rooks and destroy the nests where they had chosen to take them. The seeming act of vandalism was perhaps justified by his hope that the birds, of which he was clearly very fond, would be enticed back to their former home. The nests were destroyed two or three times but the rooks refused to return. They gathered up the remains of the nests that were strewn on the ground, and rebuilt their nests on the trees which they now regarded as their new home. When it was clear that the birds had no intention of ever returning, the owner gave up. The servant, who had tried to get the birds to return, was not surprised when the ill-fortune, which he had foreseen by the desertion of the birds, struck his master not long afterwards. There was a widespread belief at this time — and indeed such may continue to the present day — that terrible ill-luck would fall upon the owner of a property which had been deserted by rooks in such a seemingly inexplicable way.

*The cuckoo (*y Gog*)*

Moving on to the cuckoo, that strange bird beloved of lovers, there are many legends and varied opinions concerning its habits and its chanting of 'cuckoo, cuckoo' for hours on end during the early summer months. Its habit, as is well known, of appropriating the nest of another bird in order to lay its own egg and its ruthlessness in forcing out any nestlings it may find already installed there arouses mixed feelings in people. Even its call, which sounds so sweet to those who love it and who are themselves in love, can be jarring on the nerves of others less enamoured of the bird. Sadly, like so many of our migratory species its numbers and times of arrival are changing. Fewer of these birds survive the long flight from foreign lands and their sweet and solitary notes are being heard for shorter periods of time and in fewer areas. There is a great deal of folklore surrounding this strange bird and Wales must have had its full share of these tales.

The wryneck is known as *gwas y gog* and it often followed the cuckoo and helped rear the large offspring. More commonly the meadow-pipit fulfilled that rôle, but that bird too is becoming less common, as old-fashioned meadows with all their flora and fauna are themselves disappearing; hopefully, however, a more nature-orientated method of farming the land will return and with it many of the birds that have sadly lost ground to the current intensive farming practices.

Apart from its unsocial habit of nesting, the cuckoo has in all other ways remained popular and a great deal of folklore and sayings has grown up round it. One of these mentioned again by E. Owen (p.317ff) refers to the bird's useful habit of indicating to one unsure of the direction he or she should take when leaving home to try to obtain a more profitable future. The belief was that if the bird after arrival was first heard singing flying towards the east then that would indicate the direction that a person embarking on a journey should take. The same applies to the other three

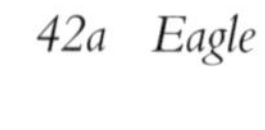

42a Eagle

points of the compass. If the cuckoo should arrive before the first hawthorn leaves open it indicates a dry year to follow and a paucity of crops. Owen records various rhymes connected with the cuckoo (p.319 ff) and the habit, which was widely believed to be true, that the cuckoo would suck birds' eggs to make room for her own as well as pitching out the fledglings. It is said that the cuckoo lays her eggs on the ground, and carries them in her beak while seeking a suitable nest in which to deposit them.

*The eagle (*eryr*)*

The eagle (**42a**) has always been regarded as king of the birds and his beauty, his stylish aerial antics, powerful beak and keen eyesight make him an impressive bird to watch. A skilful hunter, he ruthlessly descends on his prey from a considerable height and many legends were told about his courage and his powers of intimidation.

He was also associated with healing. Those who had eaten eagle's flesh were believed to be imbued with the power of healing the common disease of erysipelas. According to the belief of some Welsh people, this power remained for nine generations of the same family. In some areas it was believed that the ability to heal remained with the original healer's descendants ad infinitum. The same ability applied to the curing of shingles.

42b Kite

*The Chained Eagles of Snowdon (*Yr Wyddfa*)*

Eagles were always accredited with oracular powers and were able to foresee disasters and triumphs, peaceful outcomes and impending battles. It was possible to have some insight into their state of mind by their movements according to popular belief. When they were circling in their inimitable manner at a great height, during some crisis or battle, it indicated that victory was assured. If they flew at a low level over the rocks this indicated that the Welsh would be defeated. Sometimes when they cried ceaselessly people thought that they were experiencing the anticipation of disaster followed by mourning. Snowdon is associated with many legends over and above that of the eagles, which is not surprising with its dramatic 3561ft (1085m) height. It is believed that a stone cairn had been built over the tomb of some giant which had been slain by the legendary King Arthur. There is a lake near the summit of Snowdon called Llyn Glaslyn and alleged to be bottomless. It was supposed to be the home of a fearsome monster, the Afanc. This beast, which previously lurked in the river Conwy, was dragged by supernaturally large oxen and dropped into Llyn Glaslyn. The legend has obvious parallels to the legend of the Loch Ness monster in Inverness-shire in Scotland (*vide* Ross, *Druids* p.142 ff).

Snakes (nadredd)

It was believed by some in Wales that snakes were possessed of human understanding and could comprehend the conversation of passers-by. One story goes that in Montgomeryshire an old man told his son that once he had seen many snakes basking in the sun, as is their habit. As he passed them he said: 'I will make you jump tomorrow'. Next day, carrying a stout stick, he came to the spot where the adders had been but they had all disappeared. The following day he passed the same place but without his stick and when the adders turned furiously to attack him, he had to run for his life.

The idea of flying snakes was once known widely in Wales. Their origin was allegedly that when they had drunk a woman's milk and then eaten the consecrated bread for the holy communion, they were turned into flying serpents or dragon-like creatures, highly dangerous to man. They lurked in various places and made concerted attacks on all who dared to pass that way. One serpent's den was allegedly on the hill Moel Bentyrch; this was the location of several serpent legends. A stone pillar was erected in order to prevent the *wiber*, or winged serpent, from committing further devastation in the surrounding countryside. It was decided that the stone should be hung or covered with scarlet material which would have the effect of attracting and working the serpent up into a frenzy, as scarlet was a colour which it could not endure. Iron spikes were stuck into the stone, concealed by the red covering, in order that the hateful creature should, in attacking it, seriously wound or destroy itself on the sharp spikes, by trying to destroy the pillar. It is said to have had several lurking places in the district.

The hare (ysgyfarnog) (**43**)

The hare has always been widely regarded with superstitious awe often tempered by dislike. There are many traditions current about this delightful animal which seems to combine the qualities of both rabbit and dog. It has a bright intelligence and is often regarded as the companion of or transformation of woman to witch. The woman is often old and wizened. The animal plays an important rôle in Celtic folklore generally and there are some interesting stories and superstitions about it in the folk repertoire of Wales. One such tale is recorded in *Folk-Lore; Transactions of the Folklore Society* Vol. VII No. 4 December 1986, p.404-5. This interesting little story was contributed by one J. Bagnall Evans, Nant-yr-Eglwys, Whitland, South Wales. His father was vicar of Rhayader and the adjoining parish of Cwmtoyddwr for 23 years. One of his servants, an old man named Thomas Savage, had in his youth been a shepherd and he had amassed a large corpus of legends. One of these told how once he went with a group of people in the small hours and all were taken to a hill north of Rhayader. They were instructed to chase sheep belonging to a neighbour and drive them into one of the disused shafts

43 Brown Hare, Lepus europaeus

of a lead mine that was half full of water. While engaged in this shameful ploy, accompanied by the dogs, they suddenly became aware that there was a hare amongst them, which was joining in the 'sport'. It was more active than any of the dogs and in the words used by Evans' father, speaking of the hare: 'it was all spotted and spangled like Jacob's cattle'. The men, feeling guilty, at once ran for their lives and scattered. Evans' father used to insist that he knew it was the Devil in the form of a hare. In the same district the custom of coursing with greyhounds was current, and when the poor, hunted hare escaped they used to say: 'the old lass has got away'.

Evans also comments that universally in England, it would seem, the hare was spoken of as a female. We do not yet know the origins of the belief which identifies the hare as a witch. The spots and spangles described by the vicar's servant were 'so bright that, though the night was very dark, they lighted up dogs and sheep and everything else'. This is one of many stories told in the Celtic countries which regard the hare as having supernatural powers of transformation. For my own experience of such phenomena see *Folklore of the Scottish Highlands*, Ross, p.73 ff.

The power of turning oneself into a hare at will is considered to be hereditary in certain families in Wales. This form of enchantment is, however, held to be confined to the female sex. Rhys states that his nurse herself belonged to one of these families and was supposed to have inherited its characteristics. However few people believed in this superstition. Nevertheless in Snowdonia there is a certain valley which was not regarded as safe for Rhys to visit to question the inhabitants on the subject. This is always a delicate matter for collectors, especially when they are enquiring about 'sensitive' subjects, many of which church and chapel may disapprove. The next story deals with the hare in a more compassionate manner.

*St Monacella (*Melangell*)*

St Monacella or *Melangell*, as her name is in Welsh, was the daughter of an Irish king who wished to marry her to an Irish nobleman. Having vowed from her earliest years to retain her virginity and dedicate her life to the church, this proposed union caused her deep distress and she fled by boat to Wales and made her home in a remote and mountainous region of Powys. Her story, which now follows, is one of the most charming of all the Welsh lives of the saints. She was deeply devoted to prayer and one day while thus engaged she heard the baying of hounds and the shouting of human voices approaching her. On looking up she saw huntsmen, led by a handsome young man of noble aspect. He was, as she was to discover, Brochwel Yscythrog, Prince of Powys, pursuing a terrified hare with their hounds. The poor creature, on the point of being savaged by the dogs, who were eager for prey, ran to the beautiful young woman who was deeply engaged in prayer. It ran under her cloak and she protected it there and refused to relinquish it. When the huntsman blew his horn it stuck to his lips, making it clear that she was no ordinary person. Moved by her beauty and her courage the prince called off the hunt and approached the girl, curious to know why one so lively and evidently of noble birth was alone in this remote place. She told him that she was the daughter of a king of Ireland who had determined that she should marry an Irish prince. She, however, intended to devote her life to God and the Church. Impressed as he was by the girl's great beauty and innocence the prince immediately bestowed upon her all the land round about her and made it possible for her to create a sanctuary there and to found an abbey on the spot where he had chanced upon her. She was filled with joy and accordingly founded an abbey and lived for many years as Abbess, dying at a great age.

The hare which became her pet and symbol was never again hunted by the prince and hare-hunting was moreover prohibited throughout Powys. She was buried in the neighbouring church which was called Pennant and eventually Pennant Melangell (**44**). Today the place where her church was built and still stands retains its aura of peace and holiness. I recently visited the site and the church and was deeply moved by the sense of serenity and

44 The church of St Melangell, Powys

spirituality with which this beautiful site is imbued. In the little churchyard the quiet graves emanate their own sense of tranquillity.

It is worth noting that the churchyard of Pennant Melangell is one example of the extremely interesting circular structures which are found widely scattered in Wales. The underlying purpose of these intriguing circles would seem to have been the overcoming of ancient superstition and belief which was inevitably associated with the great stone circles and individual standing stones (*vide* chapter 6) which are scattered across the Welsh landscape and date to the Neolithic period of archaeology.

Other hare stories

Hares were always regarded as being rather special in my own family. There is something strange and almost human about their level gaze. To see a field full of hares in early spring, all drumming the ground and leaping wildly, is both an exhilarating and somewhat disturbing sight. There are numerous stories in Wales, as elsewhere in the Celtic countries of hares which are really transformed witches. They had the power both to enchant and to disenchant themselves. If one could bruise or injure them, the wound or bruise would be visible on their human forms and so would provide strong evidence against them. There are many such stories. One tells of a witch in hare form who interfered with the churn so the butter would not come (E. Owen p.229). The Rector of Llanycil was told the following story by a servant girl. When she was a servant at Drws-y-Nant near Dolgellau, the milk in the churn would not churn and there seemed to be something in the bottom of the tub, moving. The Rector, on being told this, dismissed it. However when they opened the lid a large hare leaped out and fled. This of course made everything clear — the witch herself was in the churn in the form of a hare.

This close connection of hare and witch gave a bad name to the hare because when people saw such an animal they could not be sure it was not a witch. Owen says he heard variants of the following tale in different areas of Wales. An old woman, thought to be a witch, lived in a hut in South Caernarfon, near the hilly countryside. Her grandson lived with her. Hare coursing with greyhounds — a cruel sport — was popular there and the boy used to help by startling the hare and so alerting the dogs. However the dogs never caught the hare that the grandson had started up. It was a good day's sport but it was noticed that the dogs always returned without the hare. This puzzled the hunters so much that they asked a 'wise' man what it meant. His opinion was that it was not a hare at all but a witch. He also said only a black greyhound could catch her. It was not easy to get hold of such a dog but at last one was located and bought. The chase started and they were gaining on the hare which was growing distressed. The dog began catching up with the poor creature; when she got to her own cottage and was jumping through the narrow opening in the window, the black greyhound bit her and caused her to bleed. She then sat beside the fire and started to spin and when the hunters entered the cottage only the blood on the floor and her wound gave her away. She was a witch.

Pigs

Pigs eaten at the great Celtic feasts were conveniently restored to life, whole and ready to delight the huge appetites of the warriors the next evening. Pigs were revered and devoured; the Classics comment with amazement on the number, size and long-legged build of the Belgic pigs. Kings turned into pigs; the goddess Medb's nephews eluded her in swine form. Many roads in Wales are named after pigs, especially those crossing the route of the *Twrch Trwyth*, the magical transformed swine who had swum across the sea from Ireland to Britain; his adventures are recounted in the magnificent tale, *Twrch Trwyth*. He was hunted by Arthur and was probably a boar-god in origin.

11 The declining years: summary and conclusion

With the rapidly changing nature of society on a world-wide scale and the replacement of the old ways and the pleasure taken in archaic stories and traditions, there is less attention paid to the past and the folklore and tales which typified it. Young people on the whole do not wish to remain in the 'backwaters' into which many of them were born and passed their childhood. The challenges of the city with its ready pleasures and of distant countries, which can now be reached in so comparatively short a time, have done much to render the old tales and lore superfluous, and so with the old ways. Tales which used to delight now merely irritate and the older people tend to forget stories and legends which they used to memorise after many performances by the skilled *chwedleuwyr* (storytellers), once an essential of every Welsh community. Modern values are replacing the old codes of neighbourliness and evenings spent in recounting the old ways are replaced by the lure of the television and the charm of cheap package trips by air to far distant lands. Nevertheless, a surprising amount of lore does still exist, but time is running out and is of the essence. Collecting now is a first priority for all who treasure their countreys' past and future.

Some stories, especially those attached to landscape, still linger, for example the widespread belief (by no means as fantastic as might be thought) that there are drowned cities or townships or small settlements that have been overwhelmed by waters and can still be glimpsed when the tide is low or there is little water in the reservoirs. Not all of these are purely figments of the imagination. A few miles from where we live in Wales, there are traces of submerged forests and dwellings just off the coast of Borth and Ynys-las. Over the water at Aberdovey the bells from the drowned church and village are said to ring as a warning that stormy weather is imminent. At low tide one can see the stumps of the old trees and legends about such sites still command an audience. They are both sad and exciting.

At Talley Lake, Carmarthenshire, there is believed to be a drowned settlement. This is situated close to the ruins of Talley Abbey. It is a common motif which is found widely in Wales and so strong is the oral

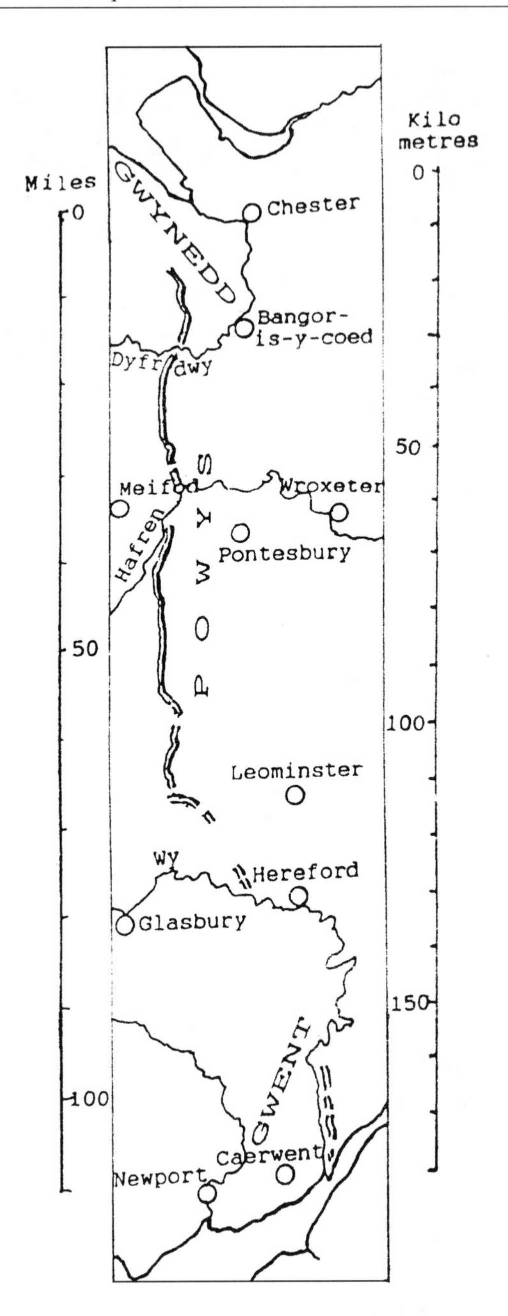

45 *Offa's Dyke* Offediche, Vallum Offae. *Constructed by Offa King of Mercia in the eighth century. From the north the Dyke leaves the Gwynedd of that day to cross the valley of the river Dyfrdwy (Dee) and then runs through Powys, crossing the valley of the river Hafren (Severn) and meeting the river Wy (Wye) before reaching the Severn Estuary to the east of Gwent*

46 *Asser, the eighth-century Welsh scholar, bishop of Sherborne and biographer of King Alfred, wrote: 'In modern times in Mercia there ruled a mighty king called Offa, who struck all the kings and regions around him with terror. He it was who ordered the great dyke to be constructed between Wales and Mercia, stretching from Sea to Sea.' Offa not only struck terror. He also struck some of the finest early medieval coins. Chris Rudd.*

tradition in all the Celtic countries that it is not impossible that some ancient legend has been handed down for generation after generation. Ultimately there may have been a crannog or lake settlement on the site.

The Hendy head (**24**) (*see also chapter 6*)

It is most unusual to find an ancient rite and tradition associated with a head cult preserved orally in the way in which the story of the Hendy head has been preserved. This remarkable stone carving formed the focal point for what we must call veneration right down to recent years and there is nothing to suggest that it has been abandoned. Indeed, the opposite would seem to be the case, and now that the people involved have decided to speak openly about it, it seems that even young people have become attracted to it. Strangely, this is still the case in remoter parts of Derbyshire and Cheshire, where the old guardians of the archaic traditions there, feeling that there is little future for traditional lore and its tabus, are more ready to speak freely about things which, after all, are part of all our unwritten history.

A leading member of the cult which centred on the Hendy head was, several years ago, courageous enough to talk about the old beliefs. Briefly, this is a summary of his account. The chief focus of the cult was Gwydion, son of Dôn, a magician in the Mabinogi of Math. The narrator recognises that those who practised the cult and were followers of Gwydion were carrying on an old Celtic form of worship. It had to be carried out in secret for fear of incurring the anger and hostility of the chapel, of which some of the participants were themselves members. This clarifies the fact that for many there was no conflict between respect for the old gods and for the Church. Gwydion, who was much associated with bardic excellence and was one of the 'three great astrologers of the island of Prydein' (Britain), had great powers of divination. In the Mabinogion he is a bard and an enchanter and he is one of the famous prisoners of Prydein; under the name of Gweir he was imprisoned in the Otherworld where he became a poet. In fact he was a seer, a prophet and, as we have seen, a poet.

In Anglesey they believed that Gwydion had three sons, namely Eog Agor, Eog Ellyll and Eog Gorach. Eog Agor was also known as Eog Altor, and he was represented by a stone head. Eog Ellyll was associated with the *Tylwyth Teg* (the fairies). Eog Gorach represented the underground or the bottom of the sea. Some people were able to communicate with these supernatural beings who were believed to inhabit another dimension. They had quite complex beliefs which are difficult to précis and to give them in full would take up far too great a share of the space available here. One important aspect of the cult was that the people in it believed they did not die but simply went through a vortex to another world: 'That's our belief . . . and you can come and go, backwards and forwards, through that vortex.' Apparently those who went through this vortex remained the same in appearance and did not age. The informant was taken to see Eog Agor, as the Hendy head was called. Its location was changed every 56 years and at that time it was in one of the outbuildings in Hendy. When I saw it, it sat impassively upon the wall of Hendy Farm and it made a very powerful impact upon me. I have seen and closely studied numerous heads of stone and other substances but I do not think I have ever come across one which so exuded latent power, and real presence.

The Anglesey cult was said to belong to the 'old' religion, which I take to be Druidism. The people in this religion believed that one could be accepted into it as children. They all had particular duties. The informant's duties were to learn the proclamations as to how to travel from one place to another following the ancient routes. These routes were exceedingly numerous and the informant found it impossible to memorise them all. The members of the cult now recognise the Celtic nature of the 'old religion'. To us the whole thing is rather complex and difficult to understand. Yet it is obvious that it has to do with ancient cults and deities which have clearly, in many areas, where there has been a long tradition of folk recitation, never been lost from the minds and memories of the people, who meet periodically to commemorate them by story and by comparanda. Strangely and unusually in the case of ancient cults and beliefs, the number of followers seems to be increasing all the time and it is, surprisingly, the young people who are now joining. They seem to be searching for their roots, and their roots lie in these ancient beliefs. The same dilemma applies to these people as it does to some of the people who have similar beliefs in other areas of Britain.

We learn that there are three very important wells in Anglesey: *Ffynnon Oer*, 'the cold well', *Ffynnon Du*, 'the black well', and *Ffynnon Marw*, 'the well of the dead'. Lakes and pools were very important in these beliefs. Ancient measurements would seem to hold a great significance for this religion and ages are calculated by the stages of the moon. Some of the information is very difficult to understand although one can always glimpse the truth which underlies it. The *stwffwl cist uffern* was a hollow tube some 4in long and made of iron, which was inserted into the mouth of the stone head. It contained a small scroll marking acceptance to the Circle, on which is written, in Welsh of course, the following:

> O Gwydion protect your servant, he who was with you in the battle of the Shores of Llifon. Keeper of the secret routes, protect him so that he might be saved from the betrayal [i.e. Christianity] so that he can return through the vortex when he is ready.
>
> He was born in the presence of the Black Well, three ages and thirteen circuits after the great crisis. This is affirmed before one hundred less fifty of the suitable sisters on the shores of the perfect lake.

After further comments and details about his own beliefs the informant ends in a somewhat moving and dignified way. When asked the question 'How do you react to people today who think that much of what you claim is just not possible?', he replied, 'This has happened to me frequently. It doesn't bother me in the slightest. If a Christian told me that Christ was crucified and arose on the third day I would say "I don't believe it!" So what? They still believe, and I believe in my religion in the same way. These are our gods, this is our belief. We do not claim to be right, we do not say that we haven't been wrong. We are ordinary people who have trodden a different path to others.'

Conclusion

The folklore of Wales is almost inexhaustible. It is a treasure-house spilling over with lore of every kind; deeply embedded Welsh traditions are inextricably entangled with the customs and beliefs, folklore and traditions of the four nations which make Ynys Prydein and the island of Ireland, our Celtic islands, what they are — a brave stronghold, a land of strict codes and a sometimes less than honourable history. But a land always true to itself. Four languages are still spoken here and we must cherish this situation which dedicated scholars and others are working so hard to preserve — fighting against a tide of technological advance and a desire to unify and so 'deculturise' our island's long and fiercely defended individuality. The Celtic languages are complex and beautiful and stem from origins now beyond recall. This singular quality is revealed in many ways, but perhaps never more so than in the prolific folklore and sophisticated literatures of Celtic Britain and Ireland.

The Welsh countryside, bounded on the east by the deep scar of the dyke built in the eighth century AD by King Offa of Mercia (**45 & 46**) — surely a strong political statement — is open, on the glorious western seaboard, to easy access from our Irish kinsmen and neighbours. In the past, there were less welcome visitations from strangers from afar, marauders and invaders, many of whom settled here and gradually became integrated into the Welsh way of life. All this belongs, however, to the troubled realms of history. This book is but an attempt to outline some small part of the rich heritage of Welsh folklore. There are still many Welsh-speaking people with their own inherited folk traditions, and the region where I live, in wild Mid-Wales, is very rich in this respect. Here the ancient oral tradition is still kept alive in teaching the ancient art of the *telyn*, harp, and the complex discipline of the *cywyddau*, Welsh alliterative verses. Each of these disciplines, and many others orally transmitted, plays a major rôle in the annual Eisteddfodau which bravely strive to keep alive the oral traditions of Wales. In this same region of Mid-Wales the evil eye can still assert its strange power and souls of the departed are yet believed to manifest themselves in bird form. The future for the Welsh tradition is thus by no means bleak and it is up to each and every one of us who live in and love Wales to make such contribution as we may to its preservation.

Bibliography

Adamnán, *Life of Columba*, ed. Reeves, W., Llanerch Publishers, 1988

Chris Barber, *More Mysterious Wales*, Paladin, 1987

G. Bentham and J.D. Hooker, *The Handbook of British Flora*, L. Reeve, Ashford, 1945

Peter C. Bartrum, *A Welsh Classical Dictionary*, The National Library of Wales, 1993

Rachel Bromwich and D. Simon Evans, *Culhwch and Olwen*, University of Wales Press, Cardiff, 1992

Rachel Bromwich, A.O.H. Jarman, Brynley F. Roberts (ed.) *The Arthur of the Welsh: the Arthurian Legend in Medieval Welsh Literature*, University of Wales Press, Cardiff, 1991

Rachel Bromwich, *Trioedd Ynys Prydein*, University of Wales Press, Cardiff, 1961 (new edition imminent)

T.M. Charles-Edwards, Morfydd E. Owen and Paul Russell (Ed.), *The Welsh King and his Court*, Pub. on behalf of the History and Law Committee of the Board of Celtic Studies, University of Wales Press, Cardiff, 2000.

Daily Express Encyclopedia, 1934, Daily Express Publications, London (9 vols.)

J.C. Davies, *Folklore of West and Mid-Wales*, Aberystwyth, 1911 and Llanerch, 1992

Folklore Myths and Legends of Britain, Reader's Digest Association Ltd, London, 1973

Folk-Lore; Transactions of the Folklore Society Vol. VII No. 4 December 1986

Gerald of Wales, *The Journey through Wales*; The Description of Wales, Penguin Classics, trans. Lewis Thorpe, 1978

Chris Grooms, *The Giants of Wales*, The Edwin Mellen Press, Lampeter, 1993

William Heist, *The Fifteen Signs Before Doomsday*, R. Holland, Byegones, Gwasg Carreg Gwalch, Capel Garmon, 1992

M.G. Jarrett, *Early Roman Campaigns in Wales*, University of Wales Press, Cardiff, 1994

Brian John, *Pembrokeshire Past and Present*, Greencroft Books, Pembrokeshire, 1995

Francis Jones, *The Holy Wells of Wales*, University of Wales Press, Cardiff, 1992

Gwyn Jones and Thomas Jones (ed.), *The Mabinogion*, Everyman's Library, 1974

T. Gwynn Jones, D.S. Brewer, *Welsh Folklore and Folk-Custom*, Rowman & Littlefleld, 1979 (reprint of 1930)

T.D. Kendrick, *The Druids*, Methuen, London, 1927

C. Kightly, *A Traveller's Guide to Places of Worship*, Routledge & Kegan Paul, 1986

MacKendrick, P., *The Mute Stones Speak*, London, 1932

James Motley, *Tales of the Cymry*, Longmans and Hughes, London, 1848

Elias Owen, *Welsh Folk-Lore*, 1887, Woodall & Minshall

Trefor M. Owen, The Celebration of Candlemas in Wales, *Folklore*, vol. 84, Autumn 1973, 238-51

Trefor M. Owen, *Welsh Folk Customs*, Gomer Press 1987

Iorwerth C. Peate, Corn ornaments, *Folklore* vol. 82, Autumn 1971, 177-84

Thomas Pennant (1726-98) *Tours in Wales* vols. 1-3, H. Humphreys, Caernarvon, 1883

John Pughe, *The Physicians of Mddvai, Meddygon Mddfi*, London 1884, Llanerch 1993

Barry Raftery, *Pagan Celtic Ireland*, Thames & Hudson Ltd. 1994

S. Rees, Dyfed, H.M.S.O. London, 1992

John Rhys, *The Hibbert lectures*, 1886, Williams and Norgate, London, 1892

Anne Ross, *Pagan Celtic Britain*, Routledge & Kegan Paul, 1967

Anne Ross, *A Traveller's Guide to Celtic Britain*, Routledge & Kegan Paul, 1985

Anne Ross, *Druids*, Tempus, 1999

Brian Shuel, *The National Trust Guide to Traditional Customs of Britain*, Webb & Bower, Exeter, 1985

P. Sims-Williams, Degrees of Celticity in Ptolemy's Names; examples from Wales, in D.N. Parson's and P. Sims-Williams, eds., *Ptolemy*, Aberystwyth 2000, 1-15

Meic Stephens (Ed.) *The Oxford Companion to the Literature of Wales* O.U.P. 1986

Tacitus, *On Britain and Germany*,Trans. Mattingley 1948, Penguin Books

Derick S. Thomson (ed.),*Companion to Gaelic Scotland*, Basil Blackwell Publishers Ltd., 1983

Marie Trevelyan, *From Snowdon to the Sea*, John Hogg, London, 1894

Reverend John Williams ab Ithel (ed.), *The Physicians of Myddfai*, translated by John Pughe and edited by the the Welsh MSS Society, Longman & Co., London, 1890

Ifor Williams (ed.), Pedeir Keinc, *y Mabinogion*, 1930, Gwasg Prifysgol Cymru, Cardiff

Index

Figure numbers in **bold**